The Hostile Takeover of Higher Education in America

How the revolution in online learning can help students bypass the Cultural Marxists in academia and get real skills and jobs

"Of all the dispositions and habits which lead to political prosperity, religion and morality are indispensable supports...It is substantially true that virtue or morality is a necessary spring of popular government. The rule, indeed, extends with more or less force to every species of free government. Who that is a sincere friend to it can look with indifference upon attempts to shake the foundation of the fabric?"

- George Washington's "Farewell Address," September 19, 1796.

"We must organize the intellectuals, and use them to make Western civilization stink. Only then, after they have corrupted all its values and made life base, can we impose the dictatorship of the proletariat."

- Willi Münzenberg, "Red Millionaire" and international Communist operative.

Copyright 2016 by America's Survival, Inc. All rights are reserved worldwide. No part of this document may be reproduced, stored in a retrieval system or transmitted in any form or by any means – electronic, or otherwise, without the prior written permission of America's Survival, Inc.

America's Survival, Inc.
Cliff Kincaid, President
P.O. Box 146, Owings, MD 20736

www.usasurvival.org   443-964-8208

Introduction by Cliff Kincaid

In 2008, when America's Survival, Inc. (ASI) released FBI files and documentary evidence of Barack Obama's socialist, communist, and even terrorist connections, the liberal and most conservative media couldn't come to grips with the idea that a presidential candidate was a Marxist with Muslim sympathies. But Communist Party writer Frank Chapman confirmed the shocking truth when he wrote that Obama was a "mole" whose victory "was more than a progressive move; it was a dialectical leap ushering in a qualitatively new era of struggle." This Marxist "mole" has transformed America through socialized medicine, executive orders on illegal immigration, open borders, gender confusion, marijuana madness, defense cutbacks, and nuclear deals with Russia and Iran. Billionaire-financed "social change" movements such as "drug policy reform," Occupy Wall Street, the anti-Israel boycott and divestment movement, Black Lives Matter, and now a Student Debt Movement, also play key roles in this dialectical process of forcing "progressive" change. They are designed to promote the further "transformation" of America's place in the world, from capitalism and freedom into an international socialist order that spells the end of American exceptionalism.

Our special thanks go to "Jimmy from Brooklyn," an anti-communist researcher, who came up with the terms "Marxist Madrassas" and "Separation of Marx and State" to describe our predicament and a solution.

Table of Contents

Section One: Toward a "Separation of Marx and State," by Cliff Kincaid

The Politics of Student Debt, page 8
What is Cultural Marxism?, page 17
Replacing the Founding Fathers with Marx, page 31
The Death of Academic Freedom, page 36
From Goldwater Girl to Marxist, page 44
The Student Loan Scam, page 49
Overpaid Academic Elites, page 53
The College Cartel, page 57
Students as Revolutionary Cannon Fodder, page 62
Phony "Diversity," page 69
Red Dawn in Academia, page 72
Educating for World Government, page 82
Techniques of Brainwashing, page 88
Sexual Anarchy on Campus, page 94
Catholic Corruption at Georgetown, page 104
How Conservatives Survive in Academia, page 107

Section Two: Online Options for Today's Students, by Clifford Kincaid

Education Can Be Affordable, page 115

Section Three: The Brave New College Campus, by Dr. Tina Trent

Speech and Thought Control, page 119
The Banning of Cliff Kincaid, page 128
Surround and Destroy, But Quietly, Page 133

Academia and Dictatorships, page 139
Frivolity and Power, page 151
From "Safe Spaces" to "Campus Climate," page 159
Academic Crusade for Hate Speech Laws, page 171

Appendices

Appendix A: Statement of President Donald P. Christian on the Office of Compliance and Campus Climate, page 173

Appendix B: Letter to New Paltz faculty, staff and students, page 175

End Notes, page 178

Author Bios

America's Survival, Inc. (ASI) President **Cliff Kincaid,** a former writer for Ronald Reagan's favorite newspaper, *Human Events*, is a journalist and media critic. He held a news conference at Columbia University in New York City on April 14, 2014, to protest the journalism school awarding Pulitzer Prizes to media mouthpieces for National Security Agency (NSA) leaker and Russian agent Edward Snowden. Kincaid wrote, *Blood on His Hands: The True Story of Edward Snowden,* and co-authored *Back from the Dead: The Return of the Evil Empire*, which predicted a resurgent Russia, and *Red Jihad*, on Russia's links to global Islamic terrorism. ASI operates Roku and YouTube TV channels and provides a free mobile device app for Android and iPhones to access videos, news, and Facebook and Twitter feeds. ASI websites include SorosFiles.com, LeninandSharia.com, ReligiousLeftExposed.com, and usasurvival.org.

Clifford Kincaid is a foreign language instructor in South Korea and has been teaching in the country since August of 2014. He obtained his master's degree in professional development, with most of his study focused on human development. Clifford has his bachelor's degree in psychology with a minor in Spanish. In addition, he has successfully completed 12 MOOCs (Massive Open Online Courses) on the Coursera platform, which included courses in teaching methodology and photography among others.

Dr. Tina Trent writes about crime, political radicals, social movements, and academia. She received a degree in British and American Poetry from New College in Sarasota and a doctorate from the Institute for Women's Studies of Emory University, where she wrote about the impact of social movements and popular culture on criminal law under the tutelage of conservative, pro-life scholar Elizabeth Fox-Genovese.

Dr. Trent also spent more than a decade in Atlanta's worst neighborhoods, providing social services to refugees, troubled families, and crime victims and discovering first-hand the destruction caused by the poverty industry, an experience she describes as "the reason I'm now a practicing Catholic and social conservative."

Her work has appeared in publications such as Accuracy in Media, the *Atlanta Journal-Constitution,* the *Pittsburgh Tribune-Review, American Thinker, FrontPage, PJ Media, Real Clear Politics,* and *The New English Review*. She has published several in-depth reports for America's Survival, Inc., including on the influence of billionaire hedge fund operator George Soros. She helped the late Larry Grathwohl release a new edition of Larry's 1976 memoir, *Bringing Down America: An FBI Informer with the Weathermen,* an account of his time infiltrating the Weather Underground. Her website is tinatrent.com.

Toward a "Separation of Marx and State"

By Cliff Kincaid

The Politics of Student Debt

In his famous "Time for Choosing" speech in 1964, Ronald Reagan compared freedom to socialism. He captured the attraction of Marxism by telling a joke: "We have so many people who can't see a fat man standing beside a thin one without coming to the conclusion the fat man got that way by taking advantage of the thin one."

Whatever the reason or motivation, a survey earlier this year conducted by YouGov found that respondents younger than 30 (also known as millennials) have more favorable views of socialism than of capitalism.

Explaining the appeal, John L. Bowman writes in his book, *Socialism in America,* about "the moralizing about justice, freedom from oppression, disparity of wealth, and obligation to help others according to their needs..." But he says "the truth may be that socialists are just plain envious of those with money."

This human tendency, exploited by demagogues like Senator Bernie Sanders (I-VT), helps explain why thousands of college students and young people turned out in support of his 2016 presidential campaign. Having made bad choices in college and facing a stagnant economy producing few jobs, they were attracted by his promises of "free college" and reducing student college loan debt, provided that the "rich" pay for it.

One factor driving this support for socialism is the student debt facing the younger generation. Rather than recognize that colleges and universities have left them with expensive and useless degrees, they are being led to blame capitalism. Politicians are promising a bailout and young people are being organized to demand it. The price tag for this bailout is $1.3 trillion, the amount of student debt.

The Student Debt Movement is another phase in the "fundamental transformation" of the U.S. These activists, some of them supported by the Open Society Foundations of billionaire hedge fund operator George Soros, are calling for "debt strikes" and refusing to pay their loans. One group declares, "Alone, our debts are a burden. Together, they make us powerful."

We argue, by contrast, that a real educational revolution can free and educate our young people, return us to founding principles, and save our nation and its capitalist system. This is the only way to create jobs for young people who want to work and be productive, while developing an appreciation for conservative principles of political and economic freedom.

It's true that rising college costs are one of the biggest issues facing our nation. But there is a difference in the Republican and Democratic approaches to the problem. Republicans propose "new systems of learning" to "compete with traditional four-year colleges," while Democrats want more money for the mostly liberal or radical public colleges and universities.

At stake is whether the role of the state in higher education will be expanded or reduced. The $1.3 trillion in student debt has made the federal role in education one of the top fiscal issues in the country.

With estimates that as many as 43 million people in America have student debt, the 2016 Republican national platform declares, "Nationwide, student loan debt now exceeds credit card debt…Over 50 percent of recent college grads are unemployed or underemployed, working at jobs for which their expensive educations gave them no training. It is time to get back to basics and to higher education programs directly related to job opportunities." Citing the need for online universities, life-long learning, and work-based learning in the private sector, it declares that, "New models for acquiring advanced skills will be ever more important in the rapidly changing economy of the twenty-first century, especially in science, technology, engineering, and math."

The 2016 Democratic Party platform says "the high cost of college has required too many Americans to take out staggering student loans or put a degree out of reach entirely." It calls for "making debt-free college a reality for all Americans."

The Democratic Party believes this can be achieved mostly by new spending by the federal and state governments. "Bold new investments by the federal government, coupled with states reinvesting in higher education and colleges holding the line on costs, will ensure that Americans of all backgrounds will be prepared for the jobs and economy of the future," the Democrats say. "Democrats are unified in their strong belief that every student should be able to go to college debt-free, and working families should not have to pay any tuition to go to public colleges and universities."

How colleges should be "holding the line on costs" was not explained.

One current proposal is to make increasing use of the federal rule known as "Borrower Defense to Repayment," based on a statute buried in the U.S. Higher Education Act of 1965. It would enable students to dismiss their student loans if they were defrauded by colleges that misrepresented the value of their degrees and their ability to get jobs as a result. The federal government would then be able to go after the institutions of higher learning to recover the money lost in the claims.

Though not offered by the Obama Administration as a way to correct liberal bias in academia, the expanded rule could be used to highlight the useless nature of so many "sexual identity" and other Marxist-oriented courses that we examine in detail in this book.

Liberal or left-wing critics want desperately to avoid the issue of Marxist brainwashing in the classroom. In cooperation with the left-wing Center for Investigative Reporting, the August 2016 *Consumer Reports* published a report on student debt that blamed Wall Street and federal lending practices for ripping off students and state governments for not spending enough on state schools. It completely ignored the rising cost of higher education that is directly related to overpaid administrators and professors and useless academic departments and degrees.

Hidden in the fine print of the article was an interesting fact. While the Department of Education now offers a "College Scorecard" so students can determine graduation rates and 10-year-out-median salaries of graduates, the data does not reflect the "specific degrees you earn." As a result, students taking queer philosophy courses could be misled into thinking that graduating with a degree in this and other "sexual identity" fields of study could actually earn a living and make good money.

A new book by Charles Sykes, a senior fellow at the Wisconsin Policy Research Institute, carries the provocative title, *Fail U.: The False Promise of Higher Education.* He argues that we are seeing a "college bubble," with the cost of a college degree soaring by 1,125 percent since 1978, four times the rate of inflation, and the value of that degree increasingly questionable. He predicts the rise of online education, especially MOOCs (massive open online courses), which will burst that bubble. Comments from my son Clifford Kincaid exploring the current student debt problem, based on real-life experiences, have been incorporated in the first section of this book. He also provides a separate section on affordable options for today's students.

Changing academia is the key to changing the media and changing society. When Reed Irvine started Accuracy in Media (AIM), he recognized the role of the media in moving the U.S. to the left. He then started Accuracy in Academia (AIA), based on the recognition that colleges and universities were producing the left-wing journalists. I was drawn to journalism and then media criticism, for I studied from Curtis J. MacDougall's popular college textbook, *Interpretative Reporting,* which encouraged a form of advocacy journalism. MacDougall taught at Northwestern University. We obtained MacDougall's 319-page FBI file, showing his long association with a series of Communist Party front groups. That helped explain his praise of Fidel Castro and fear of Senator Joseph McCarthy's anti-communist investigations.

As a young journalism student, I "learned" from MacDougall's textbook that Walter Duranty of the *New York Times* was one of the great figures in the media. I later learned the truth -- that Duranty was a stooge of Soviet dictator Joseph Stalin and one of the greatest liars in the history of journalism. In fact, he helped Stalin cover up the deaths of as many as 10 million Ukrainians in a forced famine known as the Holodomor. [1] Duranty was also a notorious pervert and drug addict. S.J. Taylor writes in her book about Duranty, *Stalin's Apologist,* that Duranty and Aleister Crowley, a Satanist, participated in drug-taking Satanic orgies. During these orgies, verses were chanted, including one consisting of "Blood and semen! Blood and semen!"

One of those influenced by MacDougall, whose textbook was required for an entire generation of journalists, was his own son, Kent MacDougall. He generated some controversy in the late 1980s when he wrote two articles for the socialist *Monthly Review* about "boring from within" at the *Wall Street Journal* and the *Los Angeles Times*. He declared that Karl Marx, who had contributed to the *New York Tribune,* was his favorite journalist.

Kent MacDougall was doing the work of Antonio Gramsci, a prominent Italian communist who had said capitalism's power or "hegemony" rested in its institutions, including the media, education and the family. His approach has been called "transforming the consciousness of a society." The media have been a big part of this process.

The Russian communists had always planned for a total assault on the West, using any means necessary. And Gramsci's attack on the traditional family was not new. Frederick Engels, Marx's partner in writing the *Communist Manifesto*, wrote *The Origin of the Family, Private Property and the State*, arguing for abolition of the family unit to make way for total state control. But Gramsci's writings were very detailed. They were officially introduced to the United States in the mid-1950s by Carl Marzani, a publisher and Soviet KGB agent whose publishing house was subsidized by the KGB. (Curtis A. MacDougall's history of the Progressive Party, *Gideon's Army*, was published by Marzani as well. He had run for office on the communist-dominated Progressive Party ticket.)

Joseph A. Buttigieg, a Professor of English at the University of Notre Dame, was the editor and translator of the complete edition of Antonio Gramsci's *Prison Notebooks*. He was an endorser of the "150th Anniversary of The Communist Manifesto" conference, held in October, 1998, at Cooper Union's Great Hall in New York. The location was significant. Barack Obama would acknowledge in his book *Dreams from My Father* that he had attended "socialist conferences" (probably the Socialist Scholars Conferences) at Cooper Union in New York City. The Left Forum, which developed out of the Socialist Scholars Conference, also held conferences there.

Ex-Marxist James Burnham, awarded the Presidential Medal of Freedom by President Reagan in 1983, had warned in his 1964 book *Suicide of the West* about the double standard developing in academia regarding involvement with communist and other totalitarian groups. "Nearly all liberals believe communists should be allowed to speak on college campuses, and most liberals believe communists should be permitted to teach in college," he noted. But "there is no comparable liberal solicitude for fascists or even those belonging to what liberals like to refer to as 'the Radical right.'" He was referring to the fact that liberals thought they were opposed to fascism and Nazism. It's true that Communism was international and based on class, while fascism and Nazism were national socialist movements based on race. But George Watson, author of *The Lost Literature of Socialism,* noted that Hitler privately "acknowledged his profound debt to the Marxian tradition" and stated that "I have learned a great deal from Marxism..." Burnham understood that they all moved in the direction of centralized planning through state control of the economy and the individual. Indeed, as the Watson book explains, socialism can justify the collective extermination of people by race, ethnic or class category.

In addition to the mass murders of Stalin and Mao, we have seen Pol Pot's Marxist genocide in Cambodia after the U.S. withdrawal from Vietnam; the Jonestown massacre in 1978, when the Peoples Temple communist commune in Guyana committed "revolutionary suicide;" and the current collapse of "Socialism of the 21st Century" in Venezuela.

What is Cultural Marxism?

When I majored in philosophy at Miami University in Oxford, Ohio, before going to the University of Toledo to specialize in journalism and communications, there were several Marxist professors in the Department of Philosophy. One handout in one class consisted of images designed to show that "human advancement" occurs under a planned economy. This is how communism is seductively presented in academia.

Under the guidance of professors, students in philosophy published their own journal, *Praxis*, and the campus chapter of the Society for the Philosophical Study of Marxism held a conference featuring a representative of the German Democratic Republic (East Germany) and entitled, "Marxist Program for the Present Crisis."

When I asked about career prospects and was told a Ph.D. in philosophy might get me a job driving a taxi, I took a year off and went back to school, the University of Toledo, seeking what my father had always advised -- a "marketable skill." As it turned out, my background in philosophy was helpful in attaining a major in journalism and communications. However, journalism has been transformed by a revolution in technology. The field of higher education has been slow to embrace the same revolution.

What I had been exposed to was classical Marxism, the kind that emphasized the importance of the workers and the working class.

At a conference sponsored by my group, America's Survival, Inc., on April 21, 2015, investigative reporter James Simpson outlined the more recent history of Cultural Marxism. Key figures in the movement for Cultural Marxism were Antonio Gramsci; Georg Lukács, the Hungarian communist; Brandeis Professor Herbert Marcuse; and Communist International (COMINTERN) agent and "Red Millionaire" Willi Münzenberg, who declared:

> We must organize the intellectuals, and use them to make Western civilization stink. Only then, after they have corrupted all its values and made life base, can we impose the dictatorship of the proletariat.

The so-called "dictatorship of the proletariat" is the victory of the oppressed classes, now defined by Cultural Marxists as including the sexual minorities but excluding the traditional and mostly conservative working class.

In this context, the Brazilian philosopher and writer, Olavo de Carvalho, says every nation has an elite or aristocracy. He says that when this group goes against the traditions of their own country, rather than defending them, we see the nation begin to decline in influence and power.

These "educated" elites in America constitute the real one percent. Statistics show that only one or two percent of the population identifies itself as homosexual. Many from this group once requested "tolerance" or understanding to get into positions of power in academia, the media, and corporate culture, but are now silencing dissenting voices to their extreme agenda. Their influence was seen in the decision by the National Basketball Association (NBA) to yank the 2017 All-Star game from Charlotte, North Carolina, as punishment for a common-sense law based on biological differences that restricts women to ladies' restrooms. These elites, who celebrate and promote sexual minority status and transgender "choice," have become the new anti-science zealots and DNA deniers.

Even Pope Francis, who is sympathetic to Marxist economic theories, has drawn the line at gender choice, saying in horror, "Today children are taught this in school that one can choose one's sex!" He added, "We are living a moment of annihilation of man as [the] image of God." In an obvious reference to the United States and certain European nations, he said "very influential countries" were attempting to impose "ideological colonization" on the world. He said the "de-Christianization, the secularization of the modern world is strong."

The impact of the leading Cultural Marxist Professor Herbert Marcuse, a faculty member from 1954 to 1965 at Brandeis University, has been considerable. The campus administration continues to honor him as "one of the most influential social and political thinkers of the 20th century" and "an internationally renowned scholar who has been credited as being the father of the New Left." The 1960s "New Left" became the Weathermen and the terrorist Weather Underground.

Brandeis was called a "School for Terrorists" by Dr. H. Peter Metzger because "several of the so-called Brandeis terrorists trace their intellectual development back to classes taught there by Marxist professors like Herbert Marcuse and other America haters." Metzger had graduated from Brandeis University in 1953.

Those "Brandeis terrorists" included two female members of the Weather Underground, as well as Islamic terrorist Aafia Siddiqui, who went or graduated from Brandeis. The Weather Underground members, Susan Saxe and Katherine Power, were put on the FBI's Ten Most Wanted List and were convicted of involvement in a bank robbery and the murder of Boston Police Officer Walter A. Schroeder in 1970.

Siddiqui, known as "Lady Al Qaeda," was sentenced to 86 years in prison for trying to kill American soldiers and was implicated in other terrorist plots, including a planned "mass casualty attack" on the Empire State Building. The Islamic State or ISIS sought to trade captives for her release before 0beheading them.

It is significant that the so-called International Solidarity Movement (ISM) has found a base on many college campuses and attempts to delegitimize the democratic State of Israel, a U.S. ally. ISM has sponsored the BDS (boycotts, divestment, and sanctions) economic warfare campaign against Israel. Jewish students tend to be targets in these campaigns and have been threatened and assaulted.

The Black Lives Matter movement, blamed for demonizing and encouraging the murder of local police, is also very active on college campuses. It has recently joined the campaign against Israel, declaring the country is guilty of "genocide" and that, through foreign aid to Israel, Americans are made "complicit in the abuses committed by the Israeli government."

Summarizing the situation at Brandeis at the time, H. Peter Metzger said, "It would appear that Brandeis has been providing a friendly intellectual climate for kids wanting to become violent domestic revolutionaries, all under the guise of elevating 'social consciousness.'"

In 2014, Brandeis University rescinded its offer of an honorary degree to Ayaan Hirsi Ali, a Somali-born women's rights activist and critic of radical Islam. Hirsi Ali was accused of being "Islamophobic."

It is frightening that radical Islam, which doesn't respect women's rights and sponsors violence and terrorism, should have a special place of honor and respect on campus. But that is the state of higher education today.

In his report and PowerPoint presentation for our conference, James Simpson referred to this kind of double standard, which was associated with Marcuse, as "partisan tolerance." It was based on "an extreme arrogance that assumes they [the left] are infallible in their utopian fantasies, and have the right to impose their will on us no matter what we think."

In the last section of this book, Dr. Tina Trent explains this kind of atmosphere at SUNY New Paltz, where I was banned from campus because of the "climate" I was somehow threatening to disrupt.

Eric Owens of *The Daily Caller* reported, "At the last minute, officials at the State University of New York at New Paltz curtly canceled a planned campus debate between a notable left-wing media critic and a notable right-wing media critic because the right-wing media critic has right-wing views."

I told the Campusreform.org website, "It appears the totalitarian left is so determined to crush the conservative point of view that it had to be suppressed even when a leftist was on the same panel." However, the SUNY New Paltz administration was so embarrassed by the incident that it announced it would eventually bring me to the campus.

The idea of partisan tolerance, Simpson noted, was further developed in "community organizer" Saul Alinsky's *Rules for Radicals,* where he advised: Pick the target, freeze it, personalize it, and polarize it. Alinsky, who studied Marxist dialectics, popularized the tactic, but Marxist Professor Marcuse invented the concept. Described another way, all free speech had to be within Marxist boundaries. The Southern Poverty Law Center (SPLC) uses the tactic against conservatives standing in the way of the triumph of Cultural Marxism.

Explaining other aspects of the history of Cultural Marxism, Simpson noted that Georg Lukács inspired Felix Weil, Marxist son of a German industrialist, to create the Institute for Social Research in Frankfurt, Germany. The so-called "Frankfurt School" was dedicated to implementing Lukács and Münzenberg's cultural subversion plans that were largely implemented in academia by Marcuse and his followers. The Frankfurt School, which moved to New York City in the 1930s, called it "Critical Theory."

It was a sophisticated attack, dressed in academic jargon, on the foundations of Western society, in order to destroy the culture. An offshoot was Critical Race Theory. As Dr. Tina Trent has pointed out, Marxist Haywood Burns, a Harvard honors graduate and Yale-educated lawyer "was an early and influential proponent of Critical Race Theory, which asserts that the American legal system is essentially an instrument for perpetuating white supremacy and black oppression. Harvard Law Professor and Obama mentor Derrick Bell revered Haywood Burns as his own intellectual mentor, as did another of Obama's important academic mentors, Charles Ogletree." [2] Both Barack and Michelle Obama graduated from Harvard.

Obama, by his own admission, sought out the "Marxist professors" when he went to Occidental College, following a father-son relationship he had with his mentor, communist and suspected Soviet espionage agent Frank Marshall Davis.

Occidental College has since turned "Critical Theory and Social Justice" into an entire interdisciplinary department which examines "various bodies of theory and method—Marxism, psychoanalysis, the Frankfurt School, deconstruction, critical race studies, queer theory, feminist theory, postcolonial theory, and intersectionality—that interrogate the essentialist assumptions that underlie social identities." One course of study is described as an examination of "whiteness" in order to "deconstruct" it.

At Columbia, also attended by Obama, Whittaker Chambers wrote in *Witness* about entering the school as a conservative but leaving without his conservatism and "no religion." He came to believe that "the world we live in was dying" and that "only surgery could now save the wreckage of mankind, and that the Communist Party was history's surgeon." Eventually, of course, Chambers would choose freedom, becoming famous as an ex-communist for exposing top State Department official and United Nations founder Alger Hiss as a Soviet spy. As Chambers came to realize, Marxism is a hateful foreign ideology based on the elimination, through violence if necessary, of the bourgeois -- the middle-class owners of property. The current death toll, according to the *Black Book of Communism,* is 100 million dead.

The Cultural Marxist view, like the classic version, holds that the world moves through slavery, feudalism, capitalism, socialism and the eventual elimination of human alienation and exploitation through the utopia of communism. The role of the Marxists is to accelerate this process of development, through the exploitation of class and now sexual differences.

The Marxists see the U.S. as the leading capitalist nation that must be "transformed" into socialism on the road to communism. As Communist Party writer Frank Chapman wrote, Obama has been their "mole," affecting the transformation of the United States even as the old Soviet-funded Communist Party would openly endorse him for re-election in 2012.

Conflict and change are inevitable in life. The question is whether the political change is handled in such a way as to produce ultimate harmony and justice or manufactured artificially to incite more division and even violence. Obama's "hope and change" has been destruction and despair.

Current so-called movements for left-wing "social change" are based on a Marxist formula. Members of certain groups considered disadvantaged in some way are elevated over and above the others. Even popular causes such as "women's rights" are taken to extremes. Under the direction and influence of such Marxists as Bella Abzug, women were considered another "exploited" group to be used to further the communist agenda. Her "Red Feminism" proved to be extremely destructive to the traditional American family, especially the rights of the unborn. The death toll from abortion in the U.S. is nearly 50 million.

Marshall Rockford Goodman argued in his book, *Karla Marx and the Man-Haters,* that "Much perceived wisdom today is actually a creation of the Marxist Critical Theory" movement in academia. In other words, the "consciousness" of society has in fact been changed. That "wisdom," a consequence of the dialectical process, is that lesbianism became another form of liberation for women. Motherhood was thus dealt another blow.

Planned Parenthood, the nation's largest abortion provider, was founded by Margaret Sanger, a revolutionary socialist and anti-Christian activist who favored government programs to eliminate what she called "human weeds." The Nazis called it "life unworthy of life."

After a pilgrimage to Stalin's Russia, Sanger said, "[W]e could well take example from Russia, where birth control instruction is part of the regular welfare service of the government." She hailed the Soviet Union's abortion law, noting that Russia was probably the first country in the world to give official approval to abortion. "Russia today is the country of the liberated woman," she announced.

Interestingly, the workers who used to be considered cannon fodder for the communist revolution are today regarded with contempt by the liberals. House Minority Leader Nancy Pelosi says they believe in guns and God and oppose "gays." Barack Obama had said those Americans "cling to guns or religion."

Donald J. Trump has appealed to some of these "bitter clingers" in the "Rust Belt" who lost their jobs in the wake of international trade deals that sent manufacturing industries to other countries. In 2012, Cecil Roberts, president of the United Mine Workers, an affiliate of the AFL-CIO, had said Obama's then-EPA administrator Lisa P. Jackson had used executive branch rules and regulations to virtually destroy the coal industry. When he ran for president, Barack Obama had personally promised to bankrupt coal plants. At a town hall in West Virginia in 2016, Hillary Clinton said, "We're going to put a lot of coal miners and coal companies out of business."

It is not coincidental that these same areas of the country, most of them white, have been devastated by a heroin epidemic – heroin mostly coming from Mexico through porous borders. However, erecting a border wall is considered by the politically correct crowd to be "anti-immigrant."

What's lost in the discussion is that Karl Marx had supported free trade on a global basis because he saw its potential for destroying national sovereignty and established cultures, and opening the way for world revolution. However, despite the devastation inflicted on the "uneducated" workers and their families, many still cling to the American dream and do not appreciate the transformation of their country and culture. They are revolting against Cultural Marxism.

The book by J.B. Williams and Timothy Harrington, *Trumped: The New American Revolution,* looks at the nature of this revolt and the emergence of a new populist or nationalist movement, in opposition to the campaign to "destroy America from within."

The Tea Party movement was itself a tremendous force for social change and a reaction, in part, to the legislation that created Obamacare, a socialist health care disaster that is now on the verge of complete failure because of uncontrolled higher costs.

One academic, Gerald Friedman, a member of Democratic Socialists of America (DSA) and a professor of economics at the University of Massachusetts, Amherst, had candidly admitted during a discussion on our America's Survival TV show that Obama and his advisers knew that the Affordable Care Act would not control costs. They knew that a total federal takeover of the system, so-called single-payer, would have to take place. Ione Whitlock of Life Tree, Inc., a pro-life educational ministry, has documented how the George Soros-funded "Big Death" lobby has now taken center stage in the health care debate. Their objective, she says, is a federal bureaucracy in charge of life and death over the elderly.

This may be shocking to those students who are taught that "social change" comes exclusively from the left and moves the country in a "progressive" direction. The genocide from abortion is proof that's it's not "progressive" in any positive sense. Interestingly, many Millennials understand this. "We are the pro-life generation" placards are visible at the annual March for Life in Washington, D.C.

What's new is that while the Marxists used to be the experts in exploiting human suffering for the purposes of sparking revolution, financial hedge funds such as those run by George Soros are working hand-in-glove with them.

This is not unprecedented. College revolutionary James Kunen wrote in *The Strawberry Statement* that Big Business had sought to channel funds into student revolts in the 1960s as part of a dialectical process, "so they can look more in the center as they move to the left." He called these businessmen "the left wing of the ruling class." In addition to Soros, whose hedge fund exploits human suffering, these billionaires today include environmentalist Tom Steyer; homosexual activist Tim Gill; and anti-Second Amendment advocate Michael Bloomberg. High-tech billionaire Bill Gates has promoted the controversial federal "Common Core" educational standards and has given support to anti-Second Amendment activists.

These wealthy capitalists are undermining the system that gave them freedom and made them rich in order to merge America into a one-world international socialist system over which they hope to have global control. This is proven by the fact that so many of them financially support the United Nations and global taxes.

This drive for global governance, sometimes called a "New World Order," is underway. "Occupy World Street" is the name of another emerging movement of "social change," this time on a global level. A book by that same name and written by another hedge fund manager proposes a "Gaian World Order" based on reverence for an "Earth spirit" or Goddess called Gaia. It's an idea that was popularized by former Vice President Al Gore and constitutes a new form of state religion which holds that natural resources have to be protected for the sake of Gaia. The difference this time is that the globalists have a vehicle to bring this about – "climate change" – and a religious face, Pope Francis, to make it a reality in our lifetimes. These are powerful forces. On the America's Survival website, Catholic activist and attorney Elizabeth Yore wrote about George Soros operatives who promoted the papal climate change encyclical, *Laudato Si'*, and secured papal support for the U.N. Sustainable Development Goals and the climate change agreement in Paris.

Replacing the Founding Fathers with Marx

The emphasis on "whiteness," as an area of study, is already popular in academia, but not in the sense that the contributions of European Americans are recognized and honored. Those who believe in a "white identity" are denounced as bigots and racists. As communists Bill Ayers and Bernardine Dohrn put it in their book by the same name, history is a "race course against white supremacy." On the other hand, the Black Lives Matter movement is viewed as something to be examined in a positive manner.

Black Lives Matter, whose activists met with Obama and his top aide, Valerie Jarrett, is an organization that salutes convicted cop-killer Assata Shakur as a role model. A member of the Black Liberation Army (BLA), a group that worked with the communist terrorist Weather Underground, Assata Shakur, also known as Joanne Chesimard, killed a white New Jersey State Trooper, Werner Foerster, "execution style" by shooting him in the head as he lay wounded by gunfire, according to the State Troopers Association of New Jersey. She was convicted of murder and went to prison but escaped with the help of the Weather Underground to Cuba, where she is still being protected by the communist regime.

CNN commentator Marc Lamont Hill, a Professor of African American Studies at Morehouse College, was so devoted to Assata Shakur that the wallpaper of his Twitter page was once plastered with police photos of her. To this day, Hill still has a "letter from

Assata Shakur" on his blog, and he says, "Let us give thanks for her life and her sacrifice."

Melina Abdullah, Professor and Chair of the Department of Pan-African Studies at California State University, Los Angeles (CSULA), became a co-founder of Black Lives Matter in Los Angeles. She is a "womanist scholar-activist" who says her role in the academy "is intrinsically linked to broader struggles for the liberation of oppressed." Her website says she earned her Ph.D. from the University of Southern California in Political Science and her B.A. from Howard University in African-American Studies.

Abdullah was one of several professors who were sued by the Alliance Defending Freedom for their alleged participation in protesting and blocking access to a Young Americans for Freedom Free Speech Event in February. [3]

At New York University, Professor Frank Leon Roberts is teaching "Black Lives Matter: Race, Resistance, and Popular Protest." His required reading includes *Are Prisons Obsolete?*, by Angela Davis, the former top Communist Party official who received the Lenin Peace Prize in 1979. Her organization Critical Resistance has been funded by billionaire hedge fund operator George Soros.

"Black Lives Matter, this is what we've been waiting for," Davis said at the Brooklyn Museum in New York, where she was honored as the 2016 recipient of the Sackler Center First Award. Earlier in her career, as noted by Dr. Tina Trent, Davis had fled after guns she purchased were used in a bloody courtroom kidnapping committed by her "bodyguard" Jonathan Jackson, the younger brother of her incarcerated lover, George Jackson. A judge was kidnapped from the courthouse and murdered; 17-year old Jonathan Jackson was killed. George Jackson later died.

Trent notes that Angela Davis went on trial in 1972, after she had achieved the status of a rock star, especially in Europe, where the very fact of her trial was viewed as evidence of the racism of the American justice system. She beat the murder rap.

Speaking in Moscow, Davis, who had been on the FBI's Ten Most Wanted Fugitive List, applauded her totalitarian hosts:

> It is an expressibly wonderful feeling to be on the soil of the Soviet Union. Had it not been for the international campaign waged throughout the world, particularly in the Socialist countries and in the Soviet Union, I am certain I would never have been released from prison.

Davis, a college professor at the University of California at Santa Cruz, had studied philosophy at Brandeis under Herbert Marcuse and became a two-time candidate for vice-president on the Communist Party ticket. Later in her career, she came "out" as a lesbian. She gets speaking fees as high as $20,000 for her campus appearances.

Her speaker's bureau reports: "Professor Davis' teaching career has taken her to San Francisco State University, Mills College, and UC Berkeley. She also has taught at UCLA, Vassar, the Claremont Colleges, and Stanford University. She spent the last fifteen years at the University of California Santa Cruz where she is now Distinguished Professor Emerita of History of Consciousness, an interdisciplinary Ph.D. program, and of Feminist Studies."

One course in the History of Consciousness Department said, "Students read landmark works of classical and contemporary Marxism. Writings from Marx, Lenin, Trotsky, Lukács, Gramsci, Adorno, Benjamin, Sartre, Althusser, Anderson, Jameson, and Zizek are addressed." This is, of course, Cultural Marxism. It's called Critical Theory in academia.

In addition to faculty and classes, speakers on college campuses tend to be leftist. Michael Isikoff and Michael B. Kelley of Yahoo! News reported that former NSA analyst Edward Snowden, a modern-day Alger Hiss, is being invited to lecture students on campuses through video presentations from Russia. Snowden, whose disclosures have aided the Islamic terrorist group ISIS and Russian aggression against Ukraine, has collected more than $200,000 in fees for digital speaking appearances that have been arranged by one of the country's elite speakers' bureaus. The University of Colorado, Boulder, paid his speakers' bureau $56,000 to host a joint appearance with Snowden and Pulitzer Prize-winning author and journalist Ron Suskind, who served as moderator, on February 16, 2016, for 90 minutes. The contract stipulated that the moderator had to be approved by Snowden. Additional expenses brought the total cost to around $73,000.

Conservative students on liberal campuses do protest these outrages. I am reminded that an issue of the *Northwestern Chronicle,* the conservative student newspaper at Northwestern University (NU), had once highlighted the fact that former Communist terrorist bomber Bernardine Dohrn was an Associate Professor at the Northwestern School of Law and director of NU Law's children and Family Justice Center. "You might be scared to go to [her] class," the paper warned.

This sickness in academia has only gotten worse.

Despite examples like this, there are many good conservative colleges available. Lists of them are maintained by Young America's Foundation and *National Review.* [4] But interestingly, the *New York Times* is beginning to recognize the problem, running an article on the decline of donations to Yale, Princeton, and Amherst, apparently in response to a "campus culture" opposed to academic freedom. The paper also took note of the University of Chicago sending new students "a blunt statement opposing some hallmarks of campus political correctness."

The Death of Academic Freedom

On March 30, 2016, I was sitting on an airplane at Reagan National Airport on my way to Albany, New York. I was informed that a campus debate I was scheduled to participate in later that day had been cancelled. I was told to get off the plane and go home. I believe this is the first time on a college or university campus that a left-right debate has been cancelled because of objections to one side of the debate.

It appears the totalitarian left is so determined to crush the conservative point of view that it had to be suppressed even when a leftist was on the same panel.

My debate opponent, Jeff Cohen, the founder of Fairness & Accuracy in Reporting (FAIR), was taken aback. It was as if the far-left censors on the campus of the State University of New York (SUNY) at New Paltz didn't think he could hold up his end of the debate.

Faculty members at SUNY New Paltz led the opposition to my appearance on campus, citing a profile of me on the website of the Southern Poverty Law Center (SPLC). I was informed about this by the agent for the speakers' bureau which arranged the event. This fact was confirmed by the student newspaper.

My initial request to SUNY New Paltz under the Freedom of Information Law in New York State for documents about the cancellation of my debate was mostly rebuffed. Among other documents, they provided me a copy of my own letter to SUNY New Paltz President Donald P. Christian protesting the cancellation. (He responded to that by promising to change course and re-invite me to campus.) Of course, I already had a copy of that. I appealed this decision, asking for copies of emails from faculty and other employees that I knew existed. These were denied on grounds they were internal. However, a confidential source provided them to me. These messages prove that faculty, not students, led the effort to censor me. They were quite interesting and informative. One message was titled, "Radical Extremist Coming to Campus." Faculty members and others who had never met or contacted me said the following:

- "...the thought of this hateful man appearing on our diverse campus sent shivers up my spine."
- "I find him loathsome..."
- "...this is totally unacceptable in our diverse community."
- "...a hate monger."

What happened here is very important to understanding what is happening on college campuses. As James Simpson noted at our conference, it is the tactic of "partisan tolerance," meaning that conservative opponents of radical Islam, the gay rights agenda, or other leftist causes are considered the enemy.

Ken Silverstein, who is considered on the left, wrote about the Southern Poverty Law Center, "I feel that the Law Center is essentially a fraud and that it has a habit of casually labeling organizations as 'hate groups.'" He added, "In doing so, the SPLC shuts down debate, stifles free speech, and most of all, raises a pile of money, very little of which is used on behalf of poor people." As of March of 2010, he noted that its treasury was up to $175 million or so, "bigger than the GNP of some of the world's smaller nations." By June of 2016, it had a reserve fund, or endowment, of $301.8 million.

The profitable media strategy behind SPLC's use of the "hate" label to describe conservatives is to demonize them and convey the impression that they should not be taken seriously and are outside the mainstream. This writer was named on one SPLC list of "30 new activists heading up the radical right," when my background as a journalist has put me in the mainstream of conservative journalism and thought. That, in turn, was picked up by the Council on American Islamic Relations (CAIR), which included me on a list of "Islamophobic individuals" because of my work exposing radical Islam. The false claims are designed to silence the exercise of my First Amendment rights by convincing the media not to take my views seriously.

Ironically, the inspiration for this venom, the SPLC, has gotten into bed with extremists on the left who themselves have been monitored, investigated, and even imprisoned. Evelyn Schlatter, the deputy director of research of the Intelligence Project at the Southern Poverty Law Center, was at a Left Forum conference that also featured Lynne Stewart, the pro-terrorist lawyer freed from prison by the Obama administration, and members of the Freedom Road Socialist Organization (FRSO), a group raided by the FBI. Stewart once told *Monthly Review* magazine that Islamic terrorists were "basically forces of national liberation." This is how many on the left have viewed the Islamic terrorists. After all, they're fighting the West.

Among the organizations joining with the Southern Poverty Law Center at the Left Forum in New York City were:

- The Freedom Road Socialist Organization, a self-declared Marxist-Leninist organization raided by the FBI in 2010 because of its links to the terrorist FARC in Colombia and the Popular Front for the Liberation of Palestine, a Palestinian Marxist-Leninist terrorist group.
- The Progressive Labor Party, whose motto is "Fight For Communism."
- Red Star Publishers, described as "a small publishing company dedicated to making Marxist-Leninist literature available in print format at low cost." It is associated with the

Party of Communists USA and US Friends of The Soviet People.
- Revolution Books, "A bookstore for a radically different world," is associated with the Revolutionary Communist Party, USA, headed by former SDS leader Bob Avakian.
- Democratic Socialists of America (DSA), the largest socialist organization in the United States, and principal U.S. affiliate of the Socialist International.

The opening plenary was titled, "Capitalism and Militarism—at Humanity's Peril," and was predictably covered by Russia Today (RT) in a story headlined, "'Democracy in the US is a fraud' Left Forum debates next steps for Sanders movement." Speakers were:

- Medea Benjamin, an anti-Israel activist who co-founded Code Pink.
- Tariq Ali, a British Pakistani associated with the Marxist Washington, D.C.-based Institute for Policy Studies, who co-wrote the screenplay for the Oliver Stone film glorifying Venezuelan Marxist ruler Hugo Chavez.
- Chris Hedges, a former *New York Times* reporter who holds the distinction of being so far left that he was booed and greeted with chants of "USA" when he delivered a graduation speech on "War and Empire" at Rockford College in Illinois.

Titles of panels at the conference included:

- The Proletariat is Still the Revolutionary Class.
- Tear Down the Prison Walls!
- Intifada in America: The History of the Palestine Left in the United States.
- A Dialogue on Israel and Palestine With Tariq Ali and Norman Finkelstein.
- Animal Liberation Strategies in the Face of Indifference and Repression.
- Bully Nation: How Militaristic Capitalism Creates A Bullying Society.
- Silencing Dissent: False Accusations of Anti-Semitism Against Palestine Solidarity.
- Cuba—Political and Economic Reforms for 21st Century Socialism.
- Prison Abolition: A Movement Towards New Directions.
- Deconstructing Gender Identity Under Male Supremacy.
- Some Reflections on the Russian Revolution.
- A Call for Leninist Unity.
- Queer Immigrant Organizing for Liberation.

An advertisement in the Left Forum conference program guide proclaimed, "Time to Take Down the Wall between the Left and the Truth Movement. No Justice or Peace without Truth." This was an attempt to get more left-wingers on board the 9/11 truth movement, which claims U.S. government agents—not Muslim terrorists—were behind the September

11, 2001, terrorist attacks. A panel associated with this view argued that Islamophobia was responsible for blaming Muslims for the terrorist attacks.

It is alarming that a representative of the SPLC, a source of information for the media and the Justice Department about "extremism," would associate with a communist movement which has killed 100 million people throughout human history.

Julian Bond, who served as president and member of the board of the Southern Poverty Law Center, was a writer for *Freedomways*, which was influential in the black community for decades but was subsidized by the Soviet and Chinese Communist Parties. Bond was also deeply involved in the activities of the U.S. Peace Council, a Communist Party front.

Another fascinating aspect of this controversy is that the SPLC's Schlatter asked not to be photographed at the Left Forum, saying she had received death threats from "white supremacists." However, the SPLC targets its critics by name and organization, labeling them "hate groups" and running photographs of officers and employees so they can more easily be identified. The SPLC was implicated in the 2012 terrorist attack on the Washington, D.C. headquarters of the Family Research Council (FRC), when homosexual militant Floyd Corkins entered its offices and shot a security guard. He had intended to shoot and kill many others. An investigation found that Corkins identified his target on the website of the SPLC.

In addition to participating in the Left Forum, the SPLC's "Teaching Tolerance" project ran an article praising unrepentant communist terrorist bomber Bill Ayers as a "civil rights organizer, radical anti-Vietnam War activist, teacher and author." An "editor's note" went so far as to say that Ayers had become "a highly respected figure in the field of multicultural education."

Communists and other leftists are regarded by the SPLC as allies in the revolution to overturn the existing order.

Interestingly, Bill Ayers was invited to speak on the SUNY New Paltz campus in 2008 about "education in a democratic society." [5] The only protest came from a SUNY New Paltz alumnus who tore up his B.A. and sent it to the university president asking for reform of the institution. [6]

In her contribution to this book, Dr. Tina Trent analyzes this atmosphere in detail, especially the significance of its Orwellian "Office of Compliance and Campus Climate." Campuses such as SUNY New Paltz have truly become reeducation camps – or what we prefer to call them – Marxist Madrassas. These are models of what they want the United States to become. Some of these institutions even establish "academic" relations with communist and Arab regimes that brutally suppress dissenting voices.

From Goldwater Girl to Marxist

Former Secretary of State Hillary Clinton is another example of Marxist influence in higher education. This case deserves more study, since Mrs. Clinton's book, *Living History,* stops far short of explaining her involvement with extreme left-wing groups and individuals in league with America's enemies. It is a cover-up similar to what the Obama campaign carried out in 2008. Then, my group, America's Survival, Inc., with the assistance of conservative blogger Trevor Loudon, disclosed the role played by communist Frank Marshall Davis in developing Obama's Marxist worldview. In August 2008, we disclosed the 600-page FBI file on Davis.

Mrs. Clinton's book says that Hillary was the daughter of a staunch Republican and that, in high school, she read Senator Barry Goldwater's book, *The Conscience of a Conservative,* and wrote a term paper on the American conservative movement. She dedicated it to her parents, "who have always taught me to be an individual." She was a Goldwater supporter in 1964 and had "strong anti-Communist views," she says. She also got deeply involved in the United Methodist Church, which "opened my eyes and heart to the needs of others..." Her conservative views persisted, however, into the time that she entered Wellesley College in 1965, where she served as president of the college's Young Republicans during her freshman year. However, she says that she began having more doubts about the war against communism in Vietnam -- doubts fed by a Methodist magazine she was receiving at college, as well as reports in the *New York Times.*

At Wellesley, she wrote a 92-page senior thesis titled "There Is Only the Fight..." about the revolutionary strategies of Saul Alinsky, the community organizer. Alana Goodman, a staff writer for the *Washington Free Beacon,* found actual correspondence between Hillary Clinton and Saul Alinsky, shedding light on her early ideological development. At Yale Law School in 1969, Hillary Clinton helped organize demonstrations in favor of the violently racist Black Panthers. She served on the Board of Editors of the Yale Review of Law and Social Action, a "progressive" alternative to the school's traditional review. Its fall 1970 issue glorified the Panthers.

During the summer of 1971, Mrs. Clinton writes in her book, she was a law clerk at the Oakland firm of Treuhaft, Walker and Burnstein. "I spent most of my time working for Mal Burnstein researching, writing legal motions and briefs for a child custody case," she said. In fact, however, the public record shows that Clinton worked for Robert Treuhaft, a member of the Communist Party USA (CPUSA) and Harvard-trained lawyer for the party.

Barbara Olson's important 1999 book, *Hell to Pay: The Unfolding Story of Hillary Rodham Clinton,* reported that Mrs. Clinton operated in the "reaches of the left including Robert Treuhaft and Jessica Mitford," who had been "committed Communists" and "Stalinists." In addition to working for Treuhaft,

Mrs. Clinton had paved the way for Mitford to lobby then-Governor Bill Clinton on the death penalty issue. Olson also reported that Robert Borosage, who served as director of the Marxist Institute for Policy Studies (IPS), was "a colleague and close acquaintance" of Clinton.

Looking at her transformation, Edward Klein's book, *The Truth About Hillary*, says that Mrs. Clinton became an avid reader of a far-left Methodist Church publication called *Motive* magazine, which featured articles by Marxists and radical lesbian feminists. One article called for the "complete destruction of the whole male supremacist system." Klein examined a culture of lesbianism at Wellesley, as well as marijuana smoking, and noted that she maintained personal relationships with lesbians as she grew older.

Barbara Olson's book remains the best account of Hillary's communist connections and emergence as a "budding Leninist" who "understood the Leninist concept of acquiring, accumulating and maintaining political power at any cost." Olson was the lawyer and conservative commentator who was murdered by Islamic terrorists when the aircraft she was on, American Airlines Flight 77, was hijacked and flown into the Pentagon in the September 11, 2001, attacks. The crash killed 125 people on the ground and another 64 passengers and crew.

I interviewed Olson on December 8, 2000, when I hosted a radio show in the Washington, D.C. area. I asked her, "Do you believe that Hillary Rodham

Clinton is a Marxist?" She replied, "I believe she has a political ideology that has its roots in Marxism. In her formative years, Marxism was a very important part of her ideology...But when you look at her ideas on health and education, you see more government and less individual control. You see very little regard for families..." Olson reported, "Hillary has never repudiated her connection with the Communist movement in America or explained her relationship with two of its leading adherents."

As the scenario plays out in the 2016 presidential campaign, Mrs. Clinton was supposed to come across on the Democratic side looking like a moderate, by virtue of the fact that an open socialist, Senator Bernie Sanders, was running "to her left" for the Democratic nomination. The Clinton-Sanders show had all the earmarks of a carefully staged demonstration of the Marxist dialectic, an exercise designed to create the appearance of conflict in order to force even more radical change on the American people through Democratic Party rule.

How this is to be done was explained by Webster Tarpley, a former operative in the movement led by Lyndon H. LaRouche, an aging Marxist ideologue who served time in prison on fraud charges. In his "Left Forum" talk, "Destroy the GOP—Split the Dems," Tarpley suggested that the Sanders wing of the Democratic Party will take complete control and a "new progressive coalition" will emerge and dominate American politics for decades. He predicted Donald J. Trump would divide and destroy the

Republican Party. As part of this dialectical approach, 2016 Green Party presidential candidate Jill Stein continued to put left-wing pressure on the Democratic Party, with her education plank calling for abolishing student debt. Stein proposed that the Federal Reserve print $1.3 billion to somehow "erase" it. Sanders himself announced a new organization called "Our Revolution" to "empower a wave of progressive candidates this November."

It is significant that a prominent expert on dialectics, Marxist economist Richard Wolff, Professor Emeritus of Economics at the University of Massachusetts, Amherst, has endorsed Stein. So has DSA member Cornel West, a Professor Emeritus at Princeton University. They understand dialectical "progress" to mean a new level of socialist thinking, leading to the expansion of the state and more state control. Internationally, former Democratic Party chairman Howard Dean has said that "cooperation" between European socialists and the Democratic Party has "intensified significantly" over the last several years.

However, at a "Global Progress Conference" in 2008, President Barack Obama's pollster, Joel Benenson, had said that while Europeans are receptive to the expansion of government in their lives, in America there is an anti-government culture which prevents people from "expecting the State to solve their problems." Let's hope he's right.

The Student Loan Scam

Alan Collinge, author of *The Student Loan Scam*, notes that in 2007, the nation owed just $450 Billion in student loans. "By the time President Obama leaves office next year, the country will have added $1 trillion to its student loan tab," he says.

The scam goes far beyond financial dependency or "debt servitude," as Jill Stein calls it. The real scam is leftist domination of higher education. It is why this book makes the case that the old brick-and-mortar schools which have been taken over by the left can and should be replaced with true centers of learning that offer real academic freedom, and courses that teach marketable skills at a reduced cost. The kind of "political revolution" we need in this country is not of the socialist variety. Rather, it's a way forward that offers real learning through alternative educational institutions that provide online opportunities and career-advancement to students where they live and work. It means defunding the status quo and launching a true revolution in learning.

My oldest son Clifford has studied this issue, and has taken many online courses through accredited institutions of higher education. He notes that the Sanders proposal of "free college" would funnel students "into an expensive and inefficient system that is largely failing today's graduates." He adds, "By doing nothing to address the underlying cost increases of education, the American taxpayer could be looking at a new Medicare, with no horizon in sight for the ever-increasing costs of the program."

"Why should the American taxpayer and government continue to subsidize a failing university system?" he asks. "The costs of textbooks, tuition, and fees have all increased many multiples against inflation. Textbook prices alone have increased over 1,000 percent since 1977. Many college professors now demand that their students buy the book that they wrote. Not only this, but a new edition is released almost yearly. Even if a student wanted to get by using last year's edition, new textbooks often have an 'online key' that can only be used once, making the purchase of a new textbook essential in order to do the mandatory homework that can only be accessed online using this key."

The state schools that Sanders wants to subsidize usually include these exorbitant textbook requirements. By contrast, "other new and innovative online schools like the online American College of Education (ACE) require no textbook," he points out. "Rather, they assign readings and coursework using academic journal articles. The advantages of such an approach are two-fold for the student: they eliminate expensive textbooks and provide information that is much more up-to-date than a textbook can provide. Not only are expensive textbooks a thing of the past at ACE but so is expensive tuition—ACE offers numerous master's degrees in education for around $7,000."

Indeed, he notes that "in recent years there has been a proliferation of low and reasonable cost options for schooling, especially online. Lest there be any confusion, these are not online diploma mills. Rather, many of these are regionally-accredited, respectable institutions that offer bachelor's degrees, master's and even doctoral degrees for very reasonable costs." He cites Western Governors University as an example of an affordable, accredited university. It was founded by 19 governors of Western states in 1995 to offer affordable tuition by taking advantage of online learning technologies.

My son concludes by saying, "Forget a bachelor's in basket weaving; this university offers coursework in highly marketable areas like information technology, nursing, education, and business. Coursework for many of these programs can be completed entirely online. The programs with required field experiences can be conveniently completed in or near one's own hometown."

Not surprisingly, the Marxists want to perpetuate and even expand the current corrupt system because they control it. The Marxist Institute for Policy Studies released a column that said "the most indebted class ever" is graduating from college. "This year," said IPS figure Chuck Collins, "seven in 10 graduating seniors borrowed for their educations. Their average debt is now over $37,000 — the highest figure for any class ever." This part of his column is true. But rather than analyze the availability of cheap federal money, in the form of student loans, with the exploding cost of college, Collins proposed higher taxes on the "rich" to funnel more money into a failing system. This is the approach of Senator Sanders.

The problem, according to Collins, is that "The system is trying to squeeze you harder than any generation before you." That system is capitalism and it is run by the rich, he says. The answer, he insists, is higher taxes. They want more money for their Marxist takeover.

I was intrigued by the first comment on the IPS website that followed this Bernie Sanders-type approach to college debt. "You might want to look at the Professors and their pay as well as the administrators" was the response. "Colleges are the great bastions of liberalism and it's a system that doesn't work. If you want a degree in French Literature or some obscure Social Studies, don't complain about costs. Get a degree in something that the market will pay for."

Furthermore, it's not clear that the socialists could manage the current system even with more money. The wife of Senator Bernie Sanders was blamed for closing down a college in Vermont. Burlington College went out of business, thanks to debt incurred under the leadership of "educator" Dr. Jane Sanders. She was given a "golden parachute" worth $200,000 after putting the college in a precarious financial situation that eventually resulted in its bankruptcy.

Overpaid Academic Elites

Student debt is partly due to rising costs at colleges and universities, which are in the business not of preparing students for a real economy, but rather of re-engineering their social lives and their social views. These recruits to Marxism then vote for socialist-style candidates.

The election of Elizabeth Warren, a Harvard Law School Professor, as a Democratic Senator from Massachusetts, helped to shine some light on the high salaries being paid to liberal/left academics. ABC News reported that Warren's financial disclosure report showed that she earned a $429,981 salary as a professor at Harvard Law from 2010-2011. The report also showed that Warren earned an additional $136,946 in royalties for books she wrote, along with $133,938 in consulting fees.[7] During her Senatorial campaign and during the presidential campaign, when she endorsed Hillary Clinton, critics pointed out that she had benefited from "diversity," having claimed American Indian heritage to get one of her teaching jobs. However, she had no proof of such heritage.

As a professor, Warren was paid more than most. Quoting figures from the American Association of University Professors, the publication *Inside Higher Ed* reports, "The average professor's salary, across ranks, was $79,424. Average compensation, including benefits, was $94,162. Professors at private doctoral institutions made most, at $158,080 in salary and $197,418 total compensation."

Former Labor Secretary Robert Reich, a professor of public policy at the University of California, Berkeley, was paid $242,613 in 2013 but was scheduled to teach only one undergraduate class during the fall semester. Mark J. Perry of the American Enterprise Institute calculated that it worked out to $2,500 for each hour of lecture time that Reich would spend with students.

"Forty-six years ago when I started teaching, university faculty general taught 12 hours each academic year and advised graduate students," writes Peter Morici, a professor at the University of Maryland School of Business. "These days teaching loads of 6 and 9 hours are common, and undergraduate courses are increasingly staffed by adjunct and part-time faculty and graduate assistants who lack an adequate grasp of the disciplines they teach, pedagogical skills or facility with the English language."

Charles Sykes addressed this problem in his 1988 book, *Profscam: Professors and the Demise of Higher Education,* which argued that professors were protecting their own status in society "while cheating students, parents, taxpayers, and employers, and polluting the intellectual inheritance of society."

Spending on campus administrators is another problem. A 2010 Goldwater Institute report, "Administrative Bloat at American Universities: The Real Reason for High Costs in Higher Education," called for reducing government subsidies to colleges and universities. "We need to stop feeding the beast," it said.[8]

At the University of Maryland (UMD), Chancellor Robert Caret was given a $75,000 bonus and a $30,000 raise in a closed meeting, meaning that his base salary of $600,000 was rising to $630,000 in the next fiscal year. The decision by the Board of Regents violated the state open meetings law. [9] Caret lives in a three-story mansion set on 12.5 acres, known as the Hidden Waters estate, and is provided with a car and driver. Earlier this year the University System of Maryland requested bids from contractors for a $125,000 kitchen renovation in the mansion.

UMD president Wallace Loh received a salary of $526,590 in 2016. A $7.5 million mansion serves as the president's house and "event center."

"Million-dollar, even multimillion-dollar homes for university presidents are common across the country," noted Mike Bowler of the *Baltimore Sun.* "They're usually supplied, along with cars, country club memberships, lucrative corporate board positions (paying well into five figures) and other perks as part of a president's compensation package."[10]

Professor Peter Morici writes about spending by universities on "lavish student centers, athletic and entertainment facilities and hotel-like residence halls, big perks and high salaries for university presidents and senior administrators," as well as "armies of new bureaucrats whose educational value added is dubious."

I won a "Best Editorial" award for 1977-78 for an editorial I wrote for the University of Toledo student newspaper, *The Collegian,* questioning a plan to use student fees to expand UT's Glass Bowl football stadium. The $2.8 million proposal was designed to increase stadium size when existing seats were not being filled. The rationale was that the NCAA was going to require Division 1 schools have a stadium with a larger seating capacity.

At SUNY New Paltz, President Donald P. Christian is paid $234,473, in addition to a salary he receives for service on the board of the local utility, Central Hudson Gas and Electric. That has been estimated at between $135,000 and $145,000.

Bloomberg looked into the rising administrative costs, including for "diversity officers," and noted, "U.S. universities employed more than 230,000 administrators in 2009, up 60 percent from 1993, or 10 times the rate of growth of the tenured faculty…"

The University of Virginia has a diversity officer and offers a Queer Studies week that includes a workshop on the proper use of pronouns. An interdisciplinary program allows students to "study gender and sexualities with an emphasis on transnational perspectives."

The College Cartel

Students themselves are beginning to realize that blaming the rich is not going to pay off their debts or find them good jobs, when a big part of the problem is what Rep. Paul Ryan (R-WI) and other conservatives are calling the "college cartel." That is, a virtual monopoly has emerged, which controls access to education and feathers its own nest with academic bureaucracies that drain the financial resources of students and their parents. The system we should challenge is not capitalism. It is an academic ivory tower which exploits parents and students and funnels their money into educational bureaucracies that keep expanding and require constant infusions of more tax dollars.

The "college cartel" can also be seen in the aptitude exams, such as the ACT and SAT, required for college applications. An alternative known as the Vector Assessment of Readiness for College is now ready for testing. It is not based on Common Core.

My son Clifford examined alternatives based on his own experiences with a weak American job market and his discussions with American students who have actually fled the country to find jobs abroad. He writes, "As a teacher in South Korea, I encounter many American expats in their twenties and thirties who have large amounts of student loan debt. A recent conversation with another expat revealed that he came over to Korea because of limited U.S. job prospects and $90,000 in debt. In a few years of teaching over here, he has managed to pay it down to around $60,000. While his drive to pay down his debt is admirable, it shouldn't be the case that he will have to spend the next five plus years to pay off a degree that may never result in a decent job offer."

Many students take out massive federal loans simply because they are available. These loan programs were started with good intentions. They were designed to ensure that everyone had to the opportunity to go to a university, regardless of one's socioeconomic background. But my son points out, "The problem is that the money is offered with absolutely no guidance about the marketability or potential earning power of the intended degree. It might make sense to take out $100,000 in debt for a computer science degree. It would make much less sense to take out $100,000 for a degree in gender studies."

The federal loans directly contribute to the exploding cost of a college education. My son notes that the federal money in the form of the student loans "has only allowed universities to increase their overhead, dean count, and other superfluous administrative positions, and pass these costs on to the backs of today's graduates." As a result, "diversity" departments and officers are in place at colleges and universities around the country, even in conservative areas of the country.

He adds, "Brick and mortar universities simply could not charge $30,000 or more a year if a student had to finance the cost of college all on his own. Students would turn elsewhere -- either to more affordable online options or to trade schools that offer marketable skills. Colleges would quickly realize that their army of deans making over $100,000 a year would need a very severe haircut in order to offer affordable tuition and attract students. However, when the government makes this kind of money available with few strings attached there is simply no incentive for universities to cost costs."

One solution is to discontinue the federal student loan program and allow students to seek education loans in the private market, where they would have more of an incentive and even be required to come up with a plan to repay the money. Part of such a plan would be to make sure you're pursuing a degree or skill that has a better likelihood of getting a job. At the same time, as some conservative members of Congress insist, the ability to challenge the ability of the "college cartels" to set accreditation standards for colleges and universities has to continue. Some online educational institutions, which provide training in marketable skills at a much-reduced cost, are getting such accreditation. Amberton University and Western Governors University are examples of this trend. Students must be informed about these alternatives to the brick and mortar universities.

"If the federal student loan program is to continue," my son says, "there must be some kind of education program for the students who are taking on such debt. Many students are still told by high school counselors that they must attend university to get a good job. Not only are there many good jobs that don't require college, college is no longer a guarantee of a good job. When students do choose to go to university, they must be aware that simply picking a major and attending classes isn't enough. Choosing a marketable major and being aware of the job prospects of that major is essential." The failure to inform students about the facts of life is why 40 percent of those owing federal student loans are either not paying them back or behind on payments.

Since the government already sets certain standards for universities that accept students with federal loans, he says one option would be the requirement of a freshman seminar at these universities for all students in a federal loan program, or even all students in general. "This could provide basic marketability statistics on the student's choice of major and job prospects. Such a course could also include other essential job hunting skills like resume writing and interviewing -- things that were never offered at my university."

"People change their majors, and salaries and job prospects certainly change as the economy changes," my son points out. "However, at least providing this information assuages the moral responsibility of informing students before they take out life-changing debt. If a student still chooses a major that is not as marketable, at least they are informed of the uphill climb they may encounter when it comes time to enter the job market." He concludes, "The current system of increased debt and unmarketable majors simply cannot continue, for the students or the broader U.S. economy."

In fact, Senator Marco Rubio (R-FL) proposes that colleges tell students, before they take out loans, "how much people make when they graduate from that school with the degree that you're seeking." He asked, "Why is that important? Number one, it will probably teach you that the market for Roman philosophers has tightened significantly. So, you may not want to borrow $50,000 to be a Roman philosopher unless you're going to teach it, or go on to grad school. But, the other [point] is it's going to allow you to compare schools. It's going to allow you to look at two different schools, and say I want to major in history."

Without these reforms, proposing higher taxes and bigger government to deal with the student debt problem would apply more financial resources into a "system" that has clearly failed. We need a new approach that emphasizes accurate information about options, lower costs, and more freedom of choice.

Students as Revolutionary Cannon Fodder

The Institute for Policy Studies says, "Imagine a political movement made up of the 40 million households that currently hold $1.3 trillion in [student] debt." This is, in fact, their goal – to mobilize the students who showed up at Bernie Sanders for president rallies into a new student movement to demand even more money for academia.

Federal student loan debt has clearly subsidized the growth of what that commenter at IPS called the "great bastions of liberalism." Fields like gender or queer studies are critical to the Cultural Marxist effort to use higher education to mold the future of the country. Students turning out for Senator Bernie Sanders, who offers free college without debt, may have some of these degrees. Sanders himself certainly doesn't want to discourage students from going into these areas of "study" since they provide cannon fodder for the socialist revolution. Hence, he wants to help pay off their debts with higher taxes, the IPS "solution."

Organizing these students into such a force depends not only on Marxist faculty but communist groups active on campus and in society at large.

In my book, *The Sword of Revolution,* I listed a number of Marxist and communist parties active today in the United States:

- Democratic Socialists of America
- Communist Party USA
- The Revolutionary Communist Party
- The League of Revolutionaries for a New America
- Socialist Workers Party
- Party for Socialism and Liberation
- Party of Communists, USA
- Labor United in Class Struggle
- U.S. Friends of the Soviet People
- Workers World Party

Many of these groups are involved in the Black Lives Matter movement. The next phase of planned social unrest involves what the communists call a "new student movement." One of their new slogans is, "Education is a right. Student debt is a crime." Much work has been done in this regard by the Revolutionary Communist Party.

Like Bill Ayers and Bernardine Dohrn, Revolutionary Communist Party chairman Bob Avakian came out of the Students for a Democratic Society (SDS), the group that laid siege to college campuses before turning into the terrorist Weather Underground. Referred to by his followers as "Chairman Bob," Avakian is devoted to "the struggle for a communist world" and wrote a memoir, *From Ike to Mao and Beyond: My Journey from Mainstream America to Revolutionary Communist.*

While some may be tempted to dismiss Avakian and his group, he has the support of Princeton University's Cornel West, who declared, "Bob Avakian is a long distance runner in the freedom struggle against imperialism, racism and capitalism. His voice and witness are indispensable in our efforts to enhance the wretched of the earth." West is honorary chair of Democratic Socialists of America (DSA), whose Chicago branch backed Obama's political career from the start. He was a member of Obama's Black Advisory Council during his 2008 presidential run.

Those who think communism is dead do not understand "The Sword of Revolution," as we referred to Marxist dialectical warfare in one of our books. Marxist groups and the Democratic Party see the thousands of young people turning out for Bernie Sanders as a great organizing opportunity. Avakian in particular has been skillful in using the Marxist theory of dialectical warfare to see the potential of young people as a political force. He talks about the need to "transform the whole atmosphere and culture on campuses and among students as part of building resistance to crimes of this system and, most fundamentally, a revolution to do away with this system and its crimes." He says Marxists have to use "a systematic approach to bringing forward a radical student movement and a real revolutionary and communist current within that." While this may sound fanciful, even ludicrous, Avakian understands that there are "qualities of youth," in the sense that they want "to search out things for themselves, not wanting to be told what to think, and so on," which can be manipulated in a communist direction. This means directing them into class warfare and class struggle.

It has happened before. In the 1960s, youthful "social democrats" and students alienated from society were transformed by Marxist ideology, drugs, and sexually-promiscuous lifestyles into a dangerous revolutionary movement capable of violence. In 1968, after visiting Castro's Cuba, Mark Rudd and the SDS organized the closing of Columbia University. It was after this that Rudd went "underground" as a fugitive with Ayers and Dohrn. Like them, he later surfaced and was on a book tour in 2009 in California, where he declared that the election of Barack Obama was a major "advance" and provides an "opening" for the far-left to continue making gains. Rudd serves on the board, with Ayers and Dohrn, of the "Movement for a Democratic Society," which hopes to resurrect a "new SDS" on the college campuses.

In her "Declaration of a State of War," Bernardine Dohrn had declared marijuana and other mind-altering drugs to be weapons in the revolution. She said, "We fight in many ways. Dope is one of our weapons. The laws against marijuana mean that millions of us are outlaws long before we actually split. Guns and grass are united in the youth underground."

Members of the Weather Underground freed Timothy Leary, the former Harvard Professor, from prison in a jailbreak. He had been sentenced to prison on drug charges but was only one member of what author Don Lattin would call "The Harvard Psychedelic Club." They ran an institute at Harvard, known as the Harvard Psilocybin Project, to experiment with psychedelic drugs.

Leary had devoted much of his life to glamorizing the use of LSD, marijuana and other drugs. A professor had become an intellectual dope pusher, telling kids that it was all right to get stoned and drop out of life. In his last years he was a fixture on the college lecture circuit, still preaching the virtues of dope.

Today, students with high debt, no jobs, and no future are ripe for exploitation and experimentation with dangerous mind-altering drugs. Known as the "Choom Gang" president, a reference to his membership in a high school gang of heavy marijuana users, Obama has opened up the drug world to many of them by ordering his Justice Department not to enforce federal laws and treaties against the use and cultivation of marijuana.

While President Obama blames easy access to guns for acts of madness and death in society, it appears that easy access to high-potency marijuana and other drugs is really to blame in many of them. For example, the Boston Marathon bombers, Russian Jihadists Dzhokhar and Tamerlan Tsarnaev, were implicated in a Jewish triple murder case in which thousands of dollars' worth of marijuana and money were left covering the bodies. All three victims' throats were slashed. Dzhokhar Tsarnaev was not only a dope smoker but a dealer. In March, 2014, a 19-year-old college student jumped off a Denver hotel balcony after eating a pot cookie with 65 milligrams of marijuana's mind-altering ingredient, THC. There are literally dozens of cases like this.

Obama has implemented the soft-on-drugs policy, but George Soros has paid for it. One of the biggest causes into which Soros has poured millions of dollars is the legalization of dangerous drugs. Interestingly, his net worth rose from about $9 billion before Obama took office to over $24 billion today.

Hooking students on drugs is an abomination. But getting students hooked on federal money to take courses with little or no real economic value is also outrageous. The solution is competition for the educational institutions that are ripping off parents, students, and taxpayers in general.

My son points out, "Last year, 260,000 bachelor's degree holders were making the federal minimum wage. Add in the 200,000 associate degree holders making the minimum wage, and we're left with just short of half a million college degree holders getting a very poor return on their college investment, which includes not only tuition dollars but also two to four years of their time and associated lost wages."

The Obama Administration has examined only one part of the problem, attacking the practices of certain for-profit colleges which exploited poor students into paying big bucks for worthless degrees. That seemed like a sincere effort to fix one part of the problem. We then learned that former Deputy Education Secretary Tony Miller had joined with Obama's best friend and chair of the Barack Obama Foundation, Marty Nesbitt, in a proposal to buy one of the for-profit education giants, the University of Phoenix, after its worth had been reduced substantially. Rep. Virginia Foxx (R-NC) told the publication Politico, "It's ironic that a former senior official at the Department of Education -- an agency that has intentionally targeted and sought to dismantle the for-profit college industry -- would now take the reins at the country's largest for-profit college."

Also cashing in, former President Bill Clinton was honorary chancellor for Laureate International Universities, the world's largest for-profit college chain, and collected millions of dollars from them. Controversies followed reports about Laureate donations to the Clinton Foundation and State Department grants to a Laureate affiliate.

From the right, Peter Schweizer, author of the book *Clinton Cash*, examined this scandal. From the left, journalist Ken Silverstein referred to the Clinton Foundation as a vehicle to launder money and to enrich family friends. Yet, while posturing as a friend of students, Senator Sanders did not make an issue during the campaign about how education had become big business for the Clintons.

Phony "Diversity"

One warning that a particular college or university is in the grip of Cultural Marxism is the emphasis on "diversity."

Michael Walsh is the latest to document the pernicious influence of this Marxist strain in academia and American society at large. His book, *The Devil's Pleasure Palace: The Cult of Critical Theory and the Subversion of the West*, examines how American institutions have been taken over by Cultural Marxists. The concept of diversity, he writes, is one vehicle they have devised for getting Americans—"free individuals before God" – to sacrifice or trade away their liberty and replace human freedom with the State. "Having seized academia," he writes, "they left a legacy in the cancerous growth of 'studies' departments (gender, race, queer, whatever) that infest the modern university at the expense of classical learning. They have turned prominent institutions of what used to be called 'higher learning' into reeducation camps of lower learning, populating them with 'diversity' commissars and political officers, blunt fists in tweed jackets, sucking taxpayer money to fuel their own theory of destruction."

Dr. Paul Kengor's important book, *Takedown: From Communists to Progressives, How the Left Has Sabotaged Family and Marriage,* documents in detail the planned destruction of the religious values and

Western traditions that gave birth to our political and economic freedoms.

In a real sense, Cultural Marxism is "diversity." This is not intellectual diversity, but "diversity" that obliterates traditional and Biblical moral standards and requires acceptance of behavior and actions that used to be considered perversions. It is a pleasant-sounding notion that is deliberately designed to blind us to the damaging impact it has in real life on people and institutions.

"Diversity is probably the most powerful concept on American colleges today; it is certainly the most pervasive," writes Peter Wood in his book *Diversity: The Invention of a Concept.* Wood, a professor of anthropology at Boston University, writes in the book, published in 2003, that diversity became a "powerful new weapon in the culture wars."

It also became a legal pillar supporting affirmative action. In this sense, the concept of "diversity" is being used to mandate acceptance of people into higher education based on their ethnic backgrounds and heritage and not on merit. Wood writes that it is a "political doctrine asserting that *some* social categories deserve compensatory privileges in light of the prejudicial ways in which members of these categories have been treated in the past and the disadvantages they continue to face." Put another way, Robert Weissberg, emeritus professor of political science at the University of Illinois-Urbana, writes that colleges and universities, "...despite the explicit anti-discrimination requirements of the 1964 Civil Right Act, choose to admit less academically qualified blacks thereby discriminating against whites and Asians." [11] What's more, this is official state policy, from the Supreme Court on down. On June 23, 2016, the Supreme Court ruled in the case Fisher v. University of Texas at Austin that it is constitutional for the university to discriminate on the basis of race in its undergraduate admissions decisions, in order to further diversity.

Dr. Kengor, professor at Grove City College, says the diversity popularized on campus is "not fully diverse at all; it is very narrowly defined, restricted to ethnicity, gender, and sexual orientation, and is most assuredly not extended to where diversity should matter most at a university: intellectual diversity. Regrettably, diversity of thought, of ideas, and even of religious belief, is not the dominant spirit of the ideologically homogenous modern college. The forces of multiculturalism and 'tolerance' can be downright intolerant of beliefs they do not embrace. Really, the phrase 'diversity' is a fraud, conveying something else that violates the very meaning of the word."

I recently learned that my alma mater, the University of Toledo, like so many other state-funded colleges and universities, will be requiring diversity training for all students and staff as part of its Strategic Plan for Diversity and Inclusion. [12] None of this has anything to do with preparing students for real jobs with marketable skills.

Red Dawn in Academia

J.B. Matthews, Director of Research for the Special Committee on Un-American Activities of the U.S. House of Representatives, published "Communism and the Colleges," in May 1953. He estimated the number of professors in colleges and universities who had collaborated with communist front groups at 3,500, representing some four hundred institutions of higher learning.

The Matthews article names the names of many educators and the academic institutions they represented which served communist interests.

Matthews highlighted problems at several academic institutions. Indeed, his article followed investigations into the University of Chicago and Roosevelt College by the Illinois Seditious Activities Investigation Commission, otherwise known as the Broyles Commission, after its chairman, Republican Senator Paul Broyles. Matthews had been the "interrogator" at the proceeding.

Citing academic freedom, University of Chicago President Robert Hutchins defended the right of communists to teach in colleges and universities and claimed that, "The fact that some communists belong to, believe in, or even dominate some of the organizations to which some of our professors belong does not show that these professors are engaged in subversive activities." He suggested professors belonging to these groups were simply opposing fascism or racial discrimination.

In his "Communism and the Colleges" article, Matthews discussed Hutchins' testimony, in the context of noting he was no "academic small-fry" and had become an associate director (and the guiding force) of the Ford Foundation, where he was a custodian of "the funds of the largest foundation in human history" and launched several initiatives that had a profound impact on American education.

Going over Hutchins' testimony, Matthews noted that Hutchins had said the following, "It is not yet established that it is subversive to be a communist." Asked if a communist-front organization was part of the communist movement, Hutchins said, "No."

Despite the alleged fear generated by such investigations, the communist penetration of academia continued.

In his book, *Red Dawn in Retrospect*, Nevin Gussack commented that, in the 1980s, "the number of Marxist academics on college and universities proliferated like mushrooms in a garden after a heavy rain." An issue of the communist newspaper *The Guardian* noted in September 1983 that "There is a renaissance of Marxist studies underway. More than 400 courses on Marxist philosophy are offered in U.S. colleges; in the 1960s there were hardly any. Prestigious university publishers are increasingly bringing out books on Marx and Marxism…No doubt at least part of the reason for the revival of interest in Marx is that many of the student radicals of the 1960s are now the Marxist professors of the 1980s. Marxist critiques are written and thousands of students required to read the old master."

The "self-professed Marxist professor," Bertell Ollman at New York University, noted in 1989 that "A Marxist cultural revolution is taking place today in American universities. More and more students and faculty are being introduced to a Marxist interpretation of how capitalism works. It is a peaceful and democratic revolution; fought chiefly by books and lectures." The Open Syllabus Project lists *The Communist Manifesto* as number three in a list of the books students at the top U.S. colleges are required to read. "The Communist Manifesto is the third most taught in history, and is the top title in sociology," its review determined.[13]

But even the liberal *Washington Post* had noted that Ollman had written an article, "On Teaching Marxism and Building the Movement," which said that most students would conclude his course with a "Marxist outlook."

For my part, I was required to read Richard Bernstein's *Praxis and Action,* which took the academic analysis of Marxism one important step forward. Praxis refers to actions which shape and change the world. Hence, the "study" of Marxism can lead, under the careful guidance of Marxist professors, to its adoption. My own need and desire for a job led me out of this trap.

Ollman's 2003 book, *Dance of the Dialectic: Steps in Marx's Method,* explains how this process works. Our own book, *The Sword of Revolution and the Communist Apocalypse,* also explores the significance of dialectics. It is how Marxists conquer minds and seize power.

Edward Hunter, a foreign correspondent who watched the communists operate in many different countries, explained the Marxist approach in 1958 testimony to the House Committee on Un-American Activities. It's the idea of promoting constant change, "even in such basic conceptions as truth and falsity, good and bad," he noted. He said a "softening up process in America" was already underway that included "the liquidation of our attitudes on what we used to recognize as right and wrong, what we used to accept as absolute moral standards."

When Ollman was offered and then denied the chairmanship of the University of Maryland's department of politics and government, he did not give up. Like a true Marxist, he continued the struggle, filing an academic freedom lawsuit against the University of Maryland. He lost the case when university officials insisted he was being denied the job because of his administrative skills and not his ideology. He stayed at New York University. "Since 1970, he has given about 250 lectures on different aspects of Marxist theory in a dozen countries," his website proclaims.

One of his students, Fox News personality Sean Hannity, claims he got a bad grade because he supported Ronald Reagan's conservative ideas.

Another important Marxist scholar is Professor Gerald Horne, who holds the John J. and Rebecca Moores Chair of History and African American Studies at the University of Houston. A contributor to Communist Party USA publications such as *Political Affairs* magazine, he spoke at a March 23, 2007, event at New York University's Tamiment Library to celebrate the donation of Communist Party materials to the library. It was at that event that Horne, speaking before an audience that included Communist Party leaders, discussed then-Senator Barack Obama's relationship with a Communist Party figure in Hawaii, Frank Marshall Davis, who had died in 1987.

In that 2007 speech at Tamiment Library, entitled, "Rethinking the History and Future of the Communist Party," Horne had referred to Davis as "an African-American poet and journalist" who was "certainly in the orbit of the CP—if not a member ..." and had become a friend to Barack Obama and his family in Hawaii. Horne also noted that Obama, in his memoir, spoke "warmly of an older black poet, he identifies simply as 'Frank,' as being a decisive influence in helping him to find his present identity as an African-

American..." Of course, Davis was a long-time member of the party with a 600-page FBI file.

I interviewed Horne for America's Survival TV. He said he came across the activities of Davis while researching his book on labor unions in Hawaii, *Fighting in Paradise: Labor Unions, Racism and Communists in the Making of Modern Hawaii.*

A prolific writer, one of Horne's most recent books is *Black Revolutionary: William Patterson and the Globalization of the African-American Freedom Struggle, 2014.* Patterson was the mentor of Frank Marshall Davis. [14]

Dr. Kathryn Waddell Takara, a former University of Hawaii Professor of Interdisciplinary studies, was a friend and associate of Davis. She wrote a book, *Frank Marshall Davis: The Fire and the Phoenix,* which confirmed his Communist activities, anti-Christian views, and involvement in bizarre sex practices and "erotica." She was a radical herself, having written such "freedom poems" as "Mumia Abu Jamal: Knight for Justice," honoring the cop-killer, and "Angela Davis," paying tribute to the former Communist Party vice presidential candidate.

Frank Marshall Davis was the subject of a controversial film by Joel Gilbert, *Dreams from My Real Father*, which asserted that Davis took pornographic photos of Obama's mother, who was white, and had sex with her. Some of these photographs are included in the film, which further asserts that Davis was Obama's real father. Comparison photos of Barack Obama and Davis show striking similarities.

The controversy took on added significance in the wake of the publication by the *New York Times* on June 18, 2016, of a story about papers of Obama's reported father, the Kenyan, Barack Hussein Obama Sr. The paper said that President Obama has shown no interest in "the newly discovered documents [in the possession of the Schomburg Center for Research in Black Culture in Harlem], which included nearly two dozen of his father's letters, his transcripts from the University of Hawaii and Harvard University, and references from professors, advisers and supporters." Based on the *Times'* analysis of the documents in the possession of the Schomburg Center, it appeared that the Kenyan Obama didn't even claim the future President as his son.

The ultimate truth about Obama's "real father" may have to wait. Malik Obama, Barack's alleged half-brother, told Joel Gilbert that he wants a DNA test and believes Frank Marshall Davis is the real father. It is a subject that should be of interest to those in the media and academia who want the truth about America's first black president.

Another academic authority on communist exploitation of blacks is Mark Solomon, Professor Emeritus of History at Simmons College, who is now based at Harvard's W. E. B. Du Bois Institute for African and African American Research. One of his announced topics was, "What has Marxism contributed (or not contributed) to theories of African American liberation?" Solomon was a major figure in the Communist Party-dominated U.S. Peace Council and a member of the Soviet-front World Peace Council.

Solomon serves with Gerald Horne and Bertell Ollman on the editorial board of *Science & Society,* described as "the longest continuously published journal of Marxist scholarship, in any language, in the world."

A history of the publication says:

> In its early years, Science & Society played a unique role in providing a home for scholarship in the Marxist tradition. It attracted contributors from many countries, and was a major site of interaction among Marxist researchers in capitalist countries and those working in the Soviet Union and Eastern Europe.

Of the "leading figures in history, literature and the social sciences," who had written for the publication, Herbert Aptheker, once described as the Communist Party's "leading theoretician," is worth noting. The *Los Angeles Times* said he helped establish the foundation for "modern African American scholarship" in the U.S.

Professor Harvey Klehr, author of T*he Communist Experience in America: A Political and Social History,* noted that Herbert Aptheker joined the Communist Party in August 1939, *after* the Nazi-Soviet pact, "defended the pact, denied that antisemitism existed in the Communist world, and slandered as crypto-Nazis those who provided voluminous evidence of its existence."[15]

His daughter, Bettina Aptheker, wrote, *Intimate Politics: How I Grew Up Red, Fought for Free Speech and Became A Feminist Rebel.* She became Distinguished Professor, Feminist Critical Race & Ethnic Studies, University of California, Santa Cruz. Aptheker, who became a lesbian, revealed in her memoir that her father had sexually molested her as a young child.

Former New Leftist David Horowitz took note of Bettina Aptheker's revelations about her father in his excellent book, *One-Party Classroom: How Radical Professors at America's Top Colleges Indoctrinate Students and Undermine Our Democracy.*

The Bettina Aptheker child abuse case leads us back to Frank Marshall Davis, Obama's childhood Marxist mentor, whose communism was also marked by sexual perversion. Davis had written *Sex Rebel,* which was autobiographical and disclosed that he had sex with children. Obama wrote a poem about Davis called "Pop," with some strange lines about stains and smells on shorts. Writer Jack Cashill noted that the poem had definite "sexual overtones."

Another academic expert on blacks and communism is Maurice Jackson, a former high-ranking member of the Communist Party. He is an Associate Professor at Georgetown University, where he teaches such courses as "Black Power in America" and "Black Thinkers and Black Movements." Jackson was the 2011 "Annual Peace Day Speaker" at the Sidwell Friends Quaker School in Washington, D.C., where Obama's daughters, Sasha and Malia, were students. It has since been announced that Malia Obama, the oldest of President Barack Obama and first lady Michelle Obama's two daughters, will attend Harvard University. She was pictured puffing on what appeared to be a marijuana cigarette at the Lollapalooza festival in Chicago in July.

Jackson also appeared and spoke at an October 28, 2006, symposium in honor of James Jackson, a leader of the Communist Party. Angela Davis keynoted the event. Researcher Max Friedman brought to my attention a July 6, 1989, issue of the Communist Party *People's Daily World* noting a Maurice Jackson appearance on Howard University television, where he talked about a trip to Cuba and Soviet support for "liberation struggles." However, his official Georgetown bio simply says he now "promotes understanding between US and Cuba youth through the sport of skateboarding." [16]

Educating for World Government

It is noteworthy that Robert Hutchins, under fire for having communists on the payroll at the University of Chicago, was a member of the Committee to Frame a World Constitution, in order to push for a world government.[17] It was associated with the World Federalist Movement. The records of the Committee to Frame a World Constitution are maintained at the University of Chicago Library.

The movement for world government has become broadly accepted in academia and politics. It was given a big lift by the publication of Thomas Piketty's *Capital in the Twenty-first Century,* which proposes a global progressive annual tax on capital. Piketty is a professor at the Paris School of Economics, but his proposal is not new. A global tax has always been promoted as a way to fundamentally transform the current international system, in which the U.S. plays the dominant role, by transferring wealth from the U.S. to the rest of the world.

Then-First Lady Hillary Clinton spoke to the World Federalist Association (WFA), a group that favors a world government financed by global taxes. She gave a tribute to veteran newsman Walter Cronkite, a supporter of world government, on October 19, 1999. America's Survival posted a video of this event.

When Mrs. Clinton spoke to the WFA, she was approving an organization that, like the U.N. itself, was on the wrong side of the Cold War.

During the historic stand-off between the U.S. and the Soviet Union, the WFA collaborated with the Soviet Peace Committee, an instrument of the Soviet Communist regime. The WFA staged a "Mission to Moscow" and held several meetings with the Soviet Peace Committee for the purpose of discussing the goal of "general and complete disarmament" and "the strengthening of the United Nations."

Hillary Clinton researcher Carl Teichrib has provided me with a photo of a Hillary meeting with Cora Weiss from the May 2000 edition of "Peace Matters," the newsletter of the Hague Appeal for Peace. Weiss, a major figure in the Institute for Policy Studies, gained notoriety for organizing anti-Vietnam War demonstrations and traveling to Hanoi to meet with communist leaders. In the photo, Hillary is shown fawning over a Hague Appeal for Peace gold logo pin that Weiss is wearing.

Teichrib recalls being an observer at the 1999 World Federalist Association conference, held in association with the Hague Appeal for Peace, during which everyone in attendance was given an honorary membership into the WFA.

In the WFA booklet, "The Genius of Federation: Why World Federation is the Answer to Global Problems," the group described how a "world federation," a euphemism for world government, could be achieved by advancing "step by step toward global governance," mostly by enhancing the power and authority of U.N. agencies.

When the organization was founded in Asheville, North Carolina, in 1947, the local paper headlined the event "World Government Plan Outlined by Speakers." This event produced the United World Federalists (UWF), whose first president, Cord Meyer, Jr. (1947-1949), had served as chief of the International Organizations Division of the CIA. The UWF board included such figures as Albert Einstein, the renowned physicist who "never wavered from his basic conviction that only a world government could secure peace" but was subsequently linked to Soviet intelligence.[18]

A World Government Research Network exists, with a long list of figures from academia.[19] Foremost among them is Richard Falk, the former Princeton University Professor and veteran left-wing activist who believes in a "World Order" under the U.N. Falk wrote the foreword to David Ray Griffin's 9/11 book, *The New Pearl Harbor*, which argues that, despite the statements of eyewitnesses, a Boeing 757 (Flight 77) did not strike the Pentagon on 9/11. Falk argues in the foreword to Griffin's book that 9/11 gave rise to "the first borderless war, with no markers or victory or defeat," and that the "official" account of 9/11—that America was the target of a surprise attack by Islamic terrorists—has to be seriously questioned.[20]

"Not since the 1940s world government 'heyday,' when Einstein and other prominent figures advocated a world state to control the terrible new threat of nuclear weapons, have so many serious academics been thinking seriously about global integration," the World Government Research Network says.

None of this is surprising to this author, who has written two books on the United Nations, *Global Bondage* (1995) and *Global Taxes for World Government* (1997), and has argued that a plan for world government financed by global taxes is on track.

World government is currently being promoted on college and university campuses through "peace studies" or "peace and justice studies." The Peace and Justice Studies Association (PJSA), based at Georgetown University in Washington D.C., is "dedicated to bringing together academics, K-12 teachers, and grassroots activists to explore alternatives to violence and share visions and strategies for peacebuilding, social justice, and social change."

The group's 2015 conference featured David Cortright, the Director of Policy Studies at the University of Notre Dame's "Kroc Institute for International Peace Studies," named for Joan Kroc, widow of McDonald's founder Ray Kroc. [21] A veteran left-wing activist who has been a consultant or adviser to various United Nations agencies, he was listed as an endorser of the Soviet-front U.S. Peace Council when it held its second national conference in 1981. Cortright was then with the Committee for a

Sane Nuclear Policy. He is still associated with the Global Zero movement to eliminate nuclear weapons. This has been one of Obama's dreams since his student days at Columbia University. Joel Gilbert, director of the film, *Dreams from My Real Father,* says Obama was "likely" a member of the May 19th Communist Organization, "an above ground support group for the Weather Underground," during his time at Columbia University in the early 1980's.

Obama had written the article, "Breaking the War Mentality," about his involvement in the anti-nuclear cause on the campus of Columbia. The article attacked the "military-industrial interests" with their "billion-dollar erector sets" and agitated for a nuclear-free world. *The New York Times* noted that Obama "explored going further" than the so-called nuclear freeze movement, an effort on some U.S. campuses that was backed by the Soviet Union and designed to defeat President Reagan's defense build-up in the 1980s.

Ironically, however, Ukraine is the country where "global zero weapons" was actually achieved. It gave up its Soviet nuclear weapons after the Kremlin promised in the 1994 Budapest Memorandum to respect its territorial integrity and sovereignty. President Clinton signed the document on behalf of the United States. This opened the door to Russian's invasion of Ukraine in 2014 and Russian occupation of part of the country.

President Obama's sister -- "peace educator" Maya Soetoro-Ng -- seems to be aiming at even younger students. At our "Communism in the Classroom" conference at the National Press Club in Washington, D.C. on August 20, 2009, Professor Mary Grabar analyzed the 89th Annual Conference of the National Council for the Social Studies, a group that teaches students to become global citizens and commit themselves to "peace" and "social justice." The group has featured Soetoro-Ng at its national conferences. She served as the Director of Community Outreach and Global Learning for the Matsunaga Institute for Peace and Conflict Resolution at the University of Hawaii in Manoa.

A visiting scholar at the federally-funded U.S. Institute of Peace, she is now a member of the board of the Barack Obama Foundation, established in January 2014 to carry on "global progress."

Techniques of Brainwashing

It seems to be common knowledge that most professors are liberals. Samuel J. Abrams, a Professor of Politics at Sarah Lawrence College, wrote a July 1, 2016, column in the *New York Times* which noted that "the ranks of academia have shifted sharply leftward over the last 25 years." He wrote:

> The overall shift is undeniable. In surveys of the ideological leanings of college faculty members by the Higher Education Research Institute from 1989 through 2014, the percentage of those identifying as liberal has always outnumbered moderates and conservatives, but the data show a notable shift left in the middle of the 1990s. In 1989, roughly 40 percent of professors were moderate and 40 percent were liberal; the remaining 20 percent were conservative. By 2014, liberal identifiers jumped to 60 percent, with moderates declining to 30 percent and conservatives to just 10 percent.[22]

At our "Communism in the Classroom" Conference. Dr. Paul Kengor delivered a paper titled, "Anti-Anti-Communism and the Academy." [23] He explained, "The bias regarding communism that exists in modern academia is not one so much of pro-communism… but a very strong dislike, bordering on disgust in many cases, for anti-communism. What prevails in modern academia is more a matter of anti-anti-communism than anything else; in other words, these professors are not so much in favor of the communists, but strongly against anti-communists. "

Yet, it turned out that the prominent "progressive" historian, Howard Zinn, was a member of the Moscow-controlled and Soviet-funded Communist Party USA (CPUSA), according to his FBI file released to America's Survival, Inc. [24] Zinn, whose books are force-fed to young people on many college campuses, taught in the political science department of Boston University for 24 years, from 1964 to 1988, and was a major influence on the modern-day "progressive" movement that backed Barack Obama for president.[25]

We knew what they had planned in Obama's case, since we understood the anti-white and anti-Christian views of Frank Marshall Davis. But people didn't believe this kind of insidious "hope and change" was possible in America.

Similarly, before the Communist takeover in Cambodia, which resulted in the deaths of up to 2 million out of the total population of 7 million, State Department Foreign Service officer Kenneth Quinn had written a 40-page report predicting Pol Pot's Marxist genocide. "The problem was that virtually no one within the U.S. government believed me," he would later say.

He explained that anyone who had been a schoolteacher or a business owner or considered educated was singled out for execution. "Not only were these persons killed, but also their spouses and children. Entire families and entire classes of people, who might resist the new order, were to be eliminated," he said.

For those who survived, he said the approach was to "psychologically reconstruct" people. The process involved "stripping away, through terror and other means, the traditional bases, structures and forces which have shaped and guided an individual's life until he is left as an atomized, isolated individual unit; and then rebuilding him according to party doctrine by substituting a series of new values, organizations and ethical norms for the ones taken away."

A "professor" in the U.S. who gave up the "armed struggle" to brainwash students was Bill Ayers. His communist terrorist organization, the Weather Underground, targeted government facilities, especially police stations, with bombs and violence. The Weather Underground was the outcome of the Weatherman and the SDS, groups which disrupted educational activities on many college campuses in the name of fighting U.S. "imperialism" and openly agitating for a communist victory in the Vietnam War. Larry Grathwohl, an FBI informant in the Weather Underground, disclosed that Bill Ayers and Bernardine Dohrn, and their Weather Underground criminal gang, had plans to eliminate as many as 25 million Americans if they came to power.

Mary Grabar, a conservative Professor of English, analyzed the work of Ayers as an education professor for the University of Illinois for my group America's Survival, Inc. Her report was titled, *The Extreme Make-Over of William Ayers: How a Communist Terrorist Became a "Distinguished" Professor of Education.* Instead of planting bombs in government buildings, he was planting bombs in students' minds. These bombs were designed to destroy the history of America as a nation that has not only freed its own citizens but has freed other peoples and nations from totalitarian control, slavery and death. He was, in effect, attempting to carry out a communist revolution through educational channels.

Ayers did not intend for students to learn anything in the traditional sense. In fact, he seemed opposed to learning anything of real value about the American system or even the global economy that could help students get actual jobs. Instead, he wants them to undergo a transformation that will make them into revolutionary activists.

Grabar said that Ayers' educational philosophy of "social change" consists of "recycled Stalinist strategies of undermining American culture and education in order to bring about revolution."

Grabar offered the proof to student parents, as well as administrators, that Ayers was a direct threat to academic standards and discipline, not to mention the investment of huge amounts of money that have been predicated upon the notion that a college or university education will produce students with marketable skills.

Through the local Freedom of Information law, we obtained the curricula Ayers used at the University of Illinois. One book that was recommended reading was *Pedagogy of the Oppressed* by Paulo Freire, a Brazilian Marxist, who declared:

> This, then, is the great humanistic and historical task of the oppressed: to liberate themselves and their oppressors as well.

It turns out that the Freire book was required reading in "Raza Studies" or Mexican-American courses in the high schools in Tucson, Arizona, where students were provoked into protesting Arizona's new immigration law. Other required books were *Occupied America* by Rodolfo Acuña, a professor emeritus of Chicano studies at California State University in Northridge (CSUN), and *Prison Notebooks* by Antonio Gramsci.

Occupied America, the fifth edition, includes an image of Fidel Castro on the front cover, and Castro and Che Guevara on the back cover. It refers to white people as "gringos" and actually includes a quotation on page 323 from Jose Angel Gutierrez of the Mexican American Youth Organization (MAYO), who was angry over the cancellation of a government program. He declared, "We are fed up. We are going to move to do away with the injustice to the Chicano and if the 'gringo' doesn't get out of our way, we will stampede over him."

The apparent aim is to convince the Mexican-American youth that they are the victims of the "oppressors" – white society. *Occupied America* opened with a map of "The Mexican Republic, 1821," showing Mexico in control of the Southwest United States. Freire promises them "liberation" from the gringos.

The American Educational Research Association (AERA), which Bill Ayers served as a vice-president, included a "Paulo Freire Special Interest Group" in his honor. His wife, Bernardine Dohrn, ran the Children and Family Justice Center at Northwestern University Law School. She was a speaker at the 1998 Critical Resistance to the Prison Industrial Complex conference, where the Angela Davis group Critical Resistance was launched. Its major goal was the abolition of prisons, on the grounds that prisoners are victims of the capitalist system.

Regarding these efforts, Dr. Trent observes, "The generations of students passing through schools, particularly California's state colleges and universities, are being fed a daily diet of messaging lifted directly from Critical Resistance's action plan. To a shocking degree, political advocacy has replaced traditional learning in California classrooms."

Sexual Anarchy on Campus

In addition to Marxist brainwashing, campuses are also known for drinking, drug use, sexual promiscuity, sexual assaults, and crime in general. Visitors to almost any campus can see the blue light call boxes so students, especially women, can contact the police in emergencies.

Some false sexual assault allegations have also gotten attention, such as *Rolling Stone* magazine's now-retracted story about a rape at the University of Virginia. But the case involving a Stanford University rapist, Brock Turner, was instructive. He blamed the "party culture" on campus. Sentenced to only 6 months in jail, he said he was "surrounded by binge drinking and sexual promiscuity..." But text messages taken from Turner's phone included references to using marijuana, LSD and MDMA (ecstasy) before he came to school.

Baylor, a Baptist university with a reputation for Christian values, has been rocked by scandal. At least three football players have been charged with sexual assault since 2014. Its football coach was fired, its athletic director resigned, and the school's president, Kenneth Starr, was removed and then resigned as chancellor.

Less well known is the fact that the sexual anarchy at Penn State University (PSU), which included the sexual abuse of young boys in the football program, also featured bizarre sexual activities on campus supported by the administration.

Dr. Judith Reisman has written in detail about former Penn State President Graham Spanier, who is charged with alleged knowledge and a cover-up of former football coach Jerry Sandusky's child molestation crimes. Citing Spanier's doctoral dissertation, Reisman says he holds radical views on sexuality that stem in part from the "research" of Alfred Kinsey, the father of the sexual revolution. [26]

Reisman's book, *Kinsey: Crimes & Consequences*, proved that Kinsey was a pervert who knowingly used data from pedophiles. His dubious data was designed to create the impression that sexual promiscuity and deviancy were normal and therefore acceptable.

Kinsey, an entomologist who taught at the University of Indiana, published two pseudo-scientific books, *Sexuality in the Human Male*, and *Sexuality in the Human Female*. Accuracy in Media founder Reed Irvine noted, "His goal was to break down all the barriers to sexual activity: pre-marital chastity, marital fidelity, bans on homosexual sex and a wide range of perversions, and the taboos of incest and sex between adults and young children."

Kinsey's fraudulent data was a critical part of the sexual revolution brought on by the Cultural Marxists. Indeed, Hugh Hefner cited Kinsey's "research" when he launched his pornographic magazine *Playboy*. The magazine celebrated the use of illegal drugs such as LSD and cocaine, and Playboy money was channeled into the movements for abortion rights, homosexual rights and legalized drugs, as well as to the Democratic Party.

In the case of PSU, a "Womyn's Sex Faire" was held in February 2001. A former Pennsylvania legislator, John Lawless, attended and found it so shocking that he videotaped part of his visit. Lawless discovered that $12,000 went to two women from Washington State to come demonstrate how to perform oral sex. Lawless said he found the fair punctuated with games like Orgasm Bingo, Pin the Clitoris on the Vulva, and the Tent of Consent, set up right outside the dormitory "... with a bucket of condoms at the door. Five people went in at a time..."

Reisman reports that Spanier was asked directly if he thought the "Sex Faire" was wrong or immoral. The PSU president apologized for certain parts of the event, but maintained that the university was committed to what he termed "free speech." He added in pure Clintonesque style, "It depends on what your definition of immoral is."

Reisman also cited the case of Dr. Richard Berendzen, then President of American University in Washington, D.C., who was arrested and convicted for child-related sex abuse. Obscene phone calls to people employed in day-care or baby-sitting jobs, during which he described fantasized sexual relations with children, were traced to his private phone.

In a recent case, Ivy League Professor J. Martin Favor of Dartmouth College was sentenced on July 11 to 5 ½ years in prison after being caught with an extensive collection of child pornography. A professor at the college for 22 years, he had chaired the African and African American studies program and was also affiliated with Women's and Gender Studies.

On the federal level, where education policy is being developed, President Obama appointed Kevin Jennings to the Department of Education. Jennings was inspired to lead a life of homosexual activism by Harry Hay, a member of the Communist Party who was not only a supporter of the North American Man-Boy Love Association (NAMBLA) but a "Radical Faerie" who believed in the power of the occult. A Stalinist and Marxist until the day he died, Hay defended NAMBLA's participation in "gay rights" marches and its membership in the International Lesbian and Gay Association.

Jennings had been the founder of the Gay, Lesbian and Straight Education Network (GLSEN), a group accused of trying to convert straight teenagers into homosexuals. GLSEN sponsored a notorious conference at Tufts University, on March 25, 2000, during which students as young as 12 were given graphic instruction in bizarre homosexual sex acts. Kids were bused in from high schools across Massachusetts.

Beyond these scandals, the University of Maryland hosted a "Queer Beyond Repair" conference that included a keynote speech on the future of the sexual device known as the dildo. Kathryn Bond Stockton, Distinguished Professor of English and Associate Vice President for Equity and Diversity at the University of Utah, was the featured speaker on the topic, "Impure Thoughts and All They Birth: What Does the Dildo of the Future Look Like?"

Titles of other topics or panels at the University of Maryland event included:

- How a Girl Becomes a Ship.
- Black Queerness and Trans Bodies.
- Traveling to Dark Places: Race, Touch, and Sadomasochism.

Another speaker was Dr. Tom Roach, the coordinator for Women, Gender, and Sexuality Studies at Bryant University. It was a Friday, he reminded his audience, which means literally the "day of Frige," also named for the goddess of sex, love, and power. His PowerPoint highlighted the fact that Frige is the primary deity for Wicca, or witchcraft. Roach's panel, "Sex, Data, and the Law," and his presentation in particular, "SCOTUS Interruptus: Raiding Rentboy.com in the Wake of Obergefell v. Hodges," were wake-up calls regarding the current LGBTQ agenda.

The author of *Friendship as a Way of Life: Foucault, AIDS, and the Politics of Shared Estrangement,* Roach based much of his presentation on the work of Michel Foucault (1926–1984), a French philosopher who died of AIDS and was accused of deliberately infecting his partners with the deadly disease.

"In the mid-1970's," says the LGBT History website, "Foucault taught at the University of California, Berkeley. He became enamored with San Francisco and its liberated gay sexuality—especially the bathhouses." Foucault declared, "I think that it is politically important that sexuality be able to function … as in the bathhouses. You cease to be imprisoned in your own face, your own past, in your own identity."

Those bathhouses were notorious incubators of AIDS.

The "Queer Beyond Repair" conference was sponsored by the following:

- College of Arts and Humanities
- The Graduate School
- Office of Diversity & Inclusion
- Office of Undergraduate Studies
- School of Languages, Literatures, and Cultures
- Center for Literary and Comparative Studies
- Nathan and Jeanette Miller Center for Historical Studies

- Department of Anthropology
- Department of Communication
- Department of English
- Department of History
- Department of Sociology
- Department of Women's Studies
- The LGBT Equity Center

The Department of Women's Studies at the University of Maryland offers B.A. and Ph.D. degrees in Women's Studies, undergraduate certificates in LGBT Studies and Women's Studies, a minor in LGBT Studies, a joint minor in Black Women's Studies (with African American Studies), and a graduate certificate in Women's Studies.

It already includes 11 core faculty and more than 80 affiliate faculty. "We have grown from 232 students in 3 courses in 1971 to over 1,366 students enrolled in Women's Studies and LGBT courses for fall 2014," the department says.

One of the courses is described as follows:

> LGBT398A:
> The Queer Child taught by Jessica Vooris. This interdisciplinary course draws on psychology, literature, history, trans studies, queer theory, and childhood studies, to examine how we think about children's gender and sexuality.

Here are some of the questions to be tackled:

- Why do many assume that a feminine boy will be gay, but think that a seven-year-old is too young to self-identify as a lesbian?
- Why do parents think it is threatening to have a transgender six-year old girl share a bathroom with their children?
- What is it like to navigate elementary school as a six-year-old trans girl?

On September 16, 2016, the University of Maryland is sponsoring "Reimaging Everything: Women of Color, Feminisms, Art, Culture, and the Humanities Symposium." It is an event "inspired by the words of revolutionary Grace Lee Boggs," a Marxist who was a member of a communist splinter group called the Workers Party. Her favorite books included *C.L.R. James's Notes on Dialectics: Left Hegelianism or Marxism-Leninism?*

The New Left Project reports that she sometimes wrote under a pseudonym of "Ria Stone" and co-authored "several insightful and pioneering works of Marxist theory," including T*he Invading Socialist Society* and *State Capitalism and World Revolution.*

Some chapters in the latter include:

- The Stalinists and the Theory of State-Capitalism
- Lenin and State-Capitalism

- Rearming the Party of World Revolution

Her book, *The Next American Revolution: Sustainable Activism For the 21st Century*, is said to document how "A world dominated by America and driven by cheap oil, easy credit, and conspicuous consumption is unraveling before our eyes." Grace Lee Boggs "shows how to create the radical social change we need to confront new realities," it says.

When Boggs died, President Obama released a statement praising her as an "author, philosopher, and activist."

The Department of Women's Studies at the University of Maryland in July announced that a full-time tenure-track position has opened up for an Assistant Professor specializing in LGBTQ studies.

We don't know what the new teaching job pays, but the Search Committee Chair, Dr. LaMonda Horton-Stallings, is paid an annual $120,000 salary. We know this because the student newspaper, *The Diamondback,* published the salary guide to the state-funded university.

Horton-Stallings' first book was titled, *Mutha is Half a Word!: Intersections of Folklore, Vernacular, Myth, and Queerness in Black Female Culture.* Her latest book is, *Funk the Erotic: Transaesthetics and Black Sexual Cultures.*

We were told the successful candidate should be able to work across multiple disciplines and have expertise in one or more of the following areas:

- Critical Race, Queer, or Transgender Theory/Studies/Policy
- Disability Studies/Crip Theory
- Transnational Genders and Sexualities, esp. Masculinities Across Racial Lines
- Gender and Sexuality in Performance Studies and Visual Culture

Queer Studies has become so accepted in academia that a "Guide to the Most Progressive LGBTQ Graduate Degrees" is now being issued.

Roger Kimball's 1990 book, *Tenured Radicals: How Politics Has Corrupted Our Higher Education*, still serves as an important and early look at what he then called the "blueprint for a radical social transformation that would revolutionize every aspect of social and political life…"

As we can see, this Marxist revolution is well underway. Defunding the Marxist Madrassas and accelerating the online learning revolution are the right way to respond.

Catholic Corruption at Georgetown

At Georgetown, the oldest Catholic and Jesuit institution of higher learning in the U.S., the official teachings of the church against homosexuality have been set aside. A "Lavender Graduation" event was held in 2016, described as "a special ceremony for LGBTQ and Ally undergraduate and graduate students," in order to "acknowledge their achievements, contributions, and unique experiences at Georgetown University."

The "Lavender Graduation" event, sponsored by the campus LGBTQ Resource Center, seemed to run directly contrary to Catholic and Christian teaching on homosexuality. In the New Testament, St. Paul taught that homosexual acts are degrading and unnatural. The Catholic Catechism declares, "Basing itself on Sacred Scripture, which presents homosexual acts as acts of grave depravity, tradition has always declared that 'homosexual acts are intrinsically disordered.' They are contrary to the natural law. They close the sexual act to the gift of life. They do not proceed from a genuine affective and sexual complementarity. Under no circumstances can they be approved."

Before this eyebrow-raising event was set to occur, Georgetown University hosted Cecile Richards, president of Planned Parenthood, which is responsible for 40 percent of all reported abortions committed in the United States. The student newspaper reported that Richards spoke "by invitation" from the student-sponsored Lecture Fund, which is funded by the university, and that she spoke about "reproductive justice" and "women's reproductive rights." Regarding abortion, the Catholic Catechism declares, "Human life must be respected and protected absolutely from the moment of conception. From the first moment of his existence, a human being must be recognized as having the rights of a person -- among which is the inviolable right of every innocent being to life."

During a recent official tour of the campus, the tour leader, a Georgetown student, boasted of how the campus had featured speeches by such prominent political figures as Senator Bernie Sanders, former Secretary of State Hillary Clinton and President Barack Obama. No conservative speakers were mentioned. Sanders spoke to Georgetown on the subject of "democratic socialism." The speech was sponsored by the Georgetown Institute of Politics and Public Service, which says it is "dedicated to reconnecting young people with the idea that politics is a noble vehicle for public service."

The university launched a "Hillary Rodham Clinton Fellowship Program," and Mrs. Clinton is the Honorary Founding Chair of the Georgetown Institute for Women, Peace and Security. Georgetown is even giving awards named after the former Secretary of State, designated the "Hillary Rodham Clinton Awards for Advancing Women in Peace and Security."

Georgetown, one of many universities with an endowment of over $1 billion, is also associated with a mystical Jesuit philosopher known as Teilhard de Chardin, who tried to combine the theory of evolution with the Christian faith. Current visitors to the Intercultural Center at Georgetown University find his words prominently featured on a wall: "The Age of Nations is past. It remains for us now, if we do not wish to perish, to set aside the ancient prejudices and build the earth."

"It is that spirit that has guided Georgetown," states Georgetown President John J. DeGioia. The Teilhard de Chardin quote has been described by advocates of a New Age or post-Christian philosophy as a "global mind shift" away from nation-states to a "global community," or "global consciousness." Prospective students are openly told that they will be groomed for success as "global citizens." Ironically, the institution traces its founding to John Carroll, whose cousin, Charles Carroll, was the only Catholic signer of the Declaration of Independence.

How Conservatives Survive in Academia

There are conservative professors at major institutions, including Georgetown. A new book, *Passing on the Right: Conservative Professors in the Progressive University*, describes the "hidden world of conservative professors" through 153 interviews, as one review noted. The authors, Jon A. Shields and Joshua M. Dunn Sr., describe how conservative professors are mostly "closeted." Conservative students can easily verify this fact. One described to me how his conservative professor would make sure to close the door to his university office before talking politics.

Some of these professors teach economics, business, accounting, or political science. At considerable risk, some of them may be critiquing Marxism in their classes. C. Bradley Thompson, the BB&T Research Professor at Clemson University and the Executive Director of the Clemson Institute for the Study of Capitalism, has commented, "In my view, we should still care about Marxism precisely because so many people are still attracted to it…" Indeed, Marxism is a poison that must be studied and isolated, in the same way that Nazism is recognized as a dangerous menace to human freedom and survival.

Senator Ted Cruz (R-TX) was an Adjunct Professor at the University of Texas School of Law in Austin, having graduated with honors from Princeton University and with high honors from Harvard Law School. In a 2010 speech, Cruz reportedly said about his years at Harvard, "There were fewer declared Republicans in the faculty when we were there than Communists! There was one Republican. But there were twelve who would say they were Marxists who believed in the Communists overthrowing the United States government."

While Jane Mayer of *The New Yorker* tried to discredit the allegations, she added:

> It may be that Cruz was referring to a group of left-leaning law professors who supported what they called Critical Legal Studies, a method of critiquing the political impact of the American legal system. Professor Duncan Kennedy, for instance, a leader of the faction, who declined to comment on Cruz's accusation, counts himself as influenced by the writings of Karl Marx. But he regards himself as a social democrat, not a Communist, and has never advocated the overthrow of the U.S. government by Communists.[27]

Kennedy, the Carter Professor of General Jurisprudence at Harvard Law School, was indeed a founding member of the Critical Legal Studies movement. But it's much more that a method of critiquing the political impact of the American legal system. It is a Marxist approach to "studying" and making the law into a revolutionary weapon.

Some conservatives who go public suffer for it. Carol Swain, a black conservative professor of political science and law at Vanderbilt University, has been attacked by the Vanderbilt Administration for criticizing the Black Lives Matter movement. She is one of the stars of Dinesh D'Souza's movie, "Hillary's America," which examines the historical racism of the Democratic Party.

On our America's Survival TV show on Roku and YouTube, we interviewed Marquette University political science professor John McAdams. The administration at this Catholic University became upset with the "Marquette Warrior" blogger for exposing various embarrassments on campus, such as a mural glamorizing the cop-killer Assata Shakur, and how an instructor tried to ban "homophobic" comments. In response to his blog post on the mural, the Marquette administration had it painted over. In response to his blog post on a ban on "homophobic" comments in one class, the administration suspended and banned McAdams from campus, and then fired him.

The McAdams case demonstrates that this process of subversion has been going on too long, even at Catholic colleges, to hope for reform of the academic institutions that have been captured and rotted from within.

It is a sign of the times that when people are told that Harvard was founded by a Puritan minister and dedicated to Christ and His Church, most react by wondering if this can actually be true. The reaction is evidence that Cultural Marxism has almost succeeded in eradicating the facts about the Christian roots of American education. Going back in history, Vaughn Shatzer's 1999 book, *History of American Education,* notes, "Of the first 126 colleges formed in America, all but three were formed on Christian principles. Up until 1900 it was very rare to find a university president who was not an ordained clergyman."

During her 2016 commencement address, Harvard President Drew Faust referred to gathering near Harvard's Memorial Church, one of those "enduring symbols of Harvard's larger identity and purposes, testaments to what universities do and believe at a time when we have never needed them more." She added, "And much is at stake, for us and for the world."

This was an extraordinary statement of historical accuracy. What's more, she went on to tell the graduates that values should be a major influence in their daily lives.

She said, "For this morning's ceremony I wore the traditional Harvard presidential robe—styled on the garment of a Puritan minister and reminding us of Harvard's origins. Values were an integral part of the defining purpose of the early years of Harvard College, created to educate a learned ministry."

It's rarely mentioned these days, but the official website declares that "Memorial Church of Harvard

University is a space of grace in the center of the Yard, rooted in the good news of Jesus Christ." In fact, Harvard itself was rooted in that good news.

The real history of Harvard and other colleges is seldom mentioned in the new, modern, and secular America that we have today. But Shatzer's book tells the almost forgotten story of how Harvard and other colleges, including Princeton, Yale, William and Mary, Rutgers, and even Columbia, were based on a Christian worldview. The facts in his book are not only important but politically relevant today, as Shatzer devotes a section to Hillary Rodham Clinton's involvement in the federal takeover of America's schools. That effort today is known as Common Core.

Referring to Widener Library and Memorial Church, Harvard President Faust said, "we need the qualities that both represent, because I believe that reason and knowledge must be inflected with values, and that those of us who are privileged to be part of this community of learning bear consequent responsibilities." She continued, "Up until the end of the 1800s, most American college presidents taught a course on moral philosophy to graduating students. But with the rise of the research university in the late nineteenth and the early twentieth century, moral and ethical purposes came to be seen as at odds with the scientific thinking transforming higher education."

She added, "But in today's world, I believe it is dangerous for universities not to fully acknowledge and embrace their responsibilities to values and to service as well as to reason and discovery. There is no value-free science. There is no algorithm that writes itself. The questions we choose to ask and the research we decide to support; the standards of integrity we expect of our colleagues and students; the community we build and the model we offer: All of this is central to who we are."

The issue of "who we are" has to consider the Founding Fathers and who they were, and why America was so successful for so long.

One of them, Thomas Jefferson, is particularly fascinating because today he is regarded as having been a proponent of the "separation of church and state." In fact, while president he was chairman of the school board of the District of Columbia. One of the principal textbooks was the Bible. Jefferson hired clergy to teach classes. He founded the University of Virginia in 1817 and its official motto was a Bible verse, John 8:32, "And ye shall know the truth, and the truth shall make you free." The scripture was also inscribed on the walls inside the Rotunda.

She concluded her address by saying, "We have a very special obligation in a very difficult time. May we and the students we send forth today embrace it."

The real solution lies in an educational revolution that transfers learning to less expensive and mostly online institutions such as Amberton University, a nondenominational Christian institution. That university proclaims that its Christian commitment "does recognize its unique role in education and believes that the principles of Christianity and academic excellence run parallel, not perpendicular."

Initiatives like Amberton University represent the future and can only grow in influence. As education writer Carrie Oakley notes, "Online schools are mushrooming everywhere these days, and it's not that hard anymore to tell the genuine ones from the diploma mills." [28]

In contrast to the race-based "diversity" policies of some state-funded schools, "online education does not discriminate on any basis – age, race, color, caste, culture – when it comes to admitting students," she notes. She cites other advantages, including:

- Online education is flexible – you can choose to finish your degree as fast as or as slow as you like, you can earn while you learn, and you can schedule classes according to your convenience.
- Online education lets you do more in less time – you can take two or even more degrees simultaneously if you're able to manage the course work and keep up with your assignments and lessons.

To encourage this online revolution, we need to defund so-called "diversity" departments. In Tennessee, legislation was introduced to defund the University of

Tennessee's Office of Diversity and Inclusion, after it used state funds for a "Sex Week," for promotion of gender-neutral pronouns, and for urging "holiday parties" that did not emphasize religion or culture. Governor Bill Haslam allowed the bill to become law without his signature. In Arizona, a law known as HB 2615 was passed, declaring that state-run universities cannot establish "free speech zones" that in fact limit free speech on campus.

At the same time, we continue to press for reform in higher education, especially journalism. America's Survival, Inc. is promoting a special curriculum based on Dr. Paul Kengor's book, *All the Dupes Fit to Print: Journalists Who Have Served as Tools of Communist Propaganda.* This lesson plan suggests resources for teaching about journalism and ethics through a case study of the historical effects of media suppression of Stalin's genocide against millions of Ukrainians, known as the Holodomor.

Recognizing the fact that many are "lost in an ideological jungle," and that our "educational circles" have been penetrated by agents of Marxist psychological warfare, or dialectics, the former foreign correspondent Edward Hunter called for giving the individual "mental survival stamina." Each person, he said, "must learn what constitutes freedom, and the pitfalls that destroy it."

After catching our breath, we must redouble our efforts to give faith, hope, life, and freedom to the next generation.

Online Options for Today's Students

By Clifford Kincaid

Education Can Be Affordable

In these times of ever-increasing higher education costs, there are fortunately new collaborations that seek to make education more affordable. Innovators in the online education arena are partnering with big name universities to bring well-regarded degrees to the masses in affordable packages.

The first such program is a partnership between edX and the Massachusetts Institute of Technology. EdX (edx.org) is an online learning provider founded by Harvard and MIT that offers massive open online courses (MOOCs). EdX is now offering a MicroMasters in supply chain management. This program takes 48 weeks to complete and can make one eligible for positions in the growing field of supply chain management and logistics. The cost for the program totals around $750 plus a final exam fee. [29]

Perhaps the most unique aspect of this program is the option to apply to MIT upon completion of the Micromasters. Students who apply successfully to MIT can complete the rest of the courses required for a full master's in only five months, rather than the full ten courses it would take someone who did not complete the edX coursework. This cuts the cost of tuition in half to around $35,000, which while still expensive is certainly more affordable than the full tuition price. [30]

Furthermore, graduates of the Micromasters are not required to take a graduate admissions test like the GRE, nor are they required to have completed a bachelor's degree in a specific field like science or math.

This kind of program offers numerous benefits to the student. Not only is there the increased accessibility that all such online programs offer, but in addition it allows students to get their feet wet before committing a large amount of time and money. A student can take a class, and then decide if it's something they definitely want to pursue in the future.

Georgia Tech, Udacity (another MOOC provider), and AT&T have recently teamed up to offer an incredible deal on a computer science degree. Utilizing the concepts pioneered by MOOCs of open courses with thousands of online students, Georgia Tech is now offering their accredited and highly-regarded Master of Science in Computer Science degree online. [31]

Georgia Tech now has over 3,000 students from 86 countries enrolled in the online program. First launched in 2014, students can take coursework including courses like software architecture and database systems. One of the greatest advantages of this program is the cost: students can complete the program for around $7,000.[32]

According to the Bureau of Labor Statistics, jobs in information and computer technology are not only growing faster than other jobs, but they also pay very well. The median wage for such jobs is $81,430, much higher than the median wage of all other jobs, which stands at $36,200.

Such a program then offers numerous advantages to a potential student. As Georgia Tech states on their website, the program is "affordable, accessible, and accredited." The price tag and option to apply for financial aid means virtually anyone can afford the program. In addition, people can take the classes wherever they are in the world, and can do so confidently, knowing that the program is fully accredited.

Finally, it is worth investigating a relatively new offering from the University of Illinois Urbana-Champaign and Coursera. This is another very innovative program that makes obtaining an MBA degree affordable and accessible.

Interested students can begin by taking business courses organized by "specialization" on the Coursera website. These specializations include leadership, business and accounting, and several others [33] Each specialization costs around $500. After completing these specializations, students may apply to the full MBA program, which can be completed entirely online. The cost of completing this program through this online hybrid format is just under $22,000. This online cost of $22,000 can be compared with the cost of attending the traditional MBA program that is offered on campus. For an Illinois resident, the traditional MBA program cost is $45,630 per year. For a non-resident, that cost jumps to $57,180.

Again we see the numerous advantages of this online program over the traditional one. Illinois non-residents can not only save about $35,000 by completing the online MBA program, they can also complete the program more conveniently and choose from multiple start dates.

One would hope to see a great proliferation of partnerships similar to those above. Universities like MIT, the University of Illinois, and Georgia Tech are all very well-known and respected institutions. Their innovation in the field of online coursework should hopefully encourage other institutions to do the same.

These partnerships that offer lower-cost tuition and educational programs are a win-win for the institution and the student. The institution gains access to thousands more students around the world. In addition, many more students gain access to top-notch educational opportunities.

The Brave New College Campus

By Tina Trent, Ph.D.

Speech and Thought Control

The Departments of Justice and Education are well on their way to extending the speech repression rules and so-called "hate speech" policies that already exist within academia to the rest of society. This is a fight they are already winning on many levels, especially among youth. The belief that the government has the right to place restrictions on speech is already broadly embraced by the millennial generation. For example, a startling 40% of people between the ages of 18 – 24 believe the government should be empowered to censor speech deemed "offensive to minority groups."[34]

This normalization of speech control via indoctrination in K-12 schools and colleges and universities has been a central strategy of hate crime law activists since the 1990's, when they failed in their efforts to add pure hate speech restrictions resembling those in Europe and Canada to the hate crime laws they passed in the United States. With this failure in legislatures and the courts, they took a page from the radicals of the Sixties and turned their attentions to saturating schoolchildren with propaganda depicting conservative politics, ideas and individuals as "haters" in classrooms. They did this through the dissemination of curricula and lesson plans such as "Hate Hurts," "Teaching Tolerance," and "anti-bullying" programming that is often no more than thinly veiled, anti-conservative political agitprop.

By specifically targeting both K-12 and higher education for recent generations, the radical left has unambiguously won the culture wars of the last fifty years. Nevertheless, people must continue sending their children to college, and so a fragile détente has evolved: parents counsel their children to keep heads down and mouths shut, to avoid the "studies" programs and radical teachers, and to matriculate quietly and move on to the world of work.

However, as an emboldened Obama administration moves to conquer as much cultural territory as possible in its waning days, this détente is less effective than in past years. The academic radicals are also nothing if not more entrenched and more powerful with every passing year. As older professors retire, the professoriate in charge of hiring committees (at least in the humanities) replace them with ever more radical hires. These radicals do not want to see any student avoid their agendas and ideas. And they have powerful allies seeded throughout campus administrations and several federal agencies.

The individual leaders of this academic vanguard are frequently so ham-fisted or bizarre that they evoke laughter rather than concern. But recent, rapid victories to open women's and even girls' bathrooms to transvestite men and boys (and vice versa), coupled with recent failures by conservative activists to pass state-based religious liberty legislation protecting business owners are waking people up to an important reality: what used to be considered "campus craziness" is hardly constrained to campuses anymore.

It is crucial for the public to now come to terms with a troubling reality: the Brave New World that academicians and university administrators have been busily nurturing on campuses and in students' minds are breaking free from the confines of academia and will soon be inescapable for all of us.

Consider the term "cis-sexual." A few years ago, virtually nobody outside the tiny world of gender-studies experts had even heard of it. But now, mention of "cis-sexuality" is commonly found among the smorgasbord of sexual esoterica with which school boards in small towns must grapple as they try to conform to the latest federal dictates regarding transgender bathrooms for sixth graders and bi-sexual locker rooms for teenagers.

"Cis," a liberal slur invented just a few years ago by gender scholars to "destabilize the hetero-normativity of identifying with the sexuality with which you are born" now must be understood by school board members scrambling to find the money to change bathroom signs as the federal government threatens to pull its funding for failing to accommodate the sex police quickly enough.

On May 13, the Federal Departments of Justice and Education issued joint directives threatening states with the loss of federal funding if they did not conform to the Obama administration's own rapidly evolving standards regarding use of gender-specific bathrooms by children and adults of different genders.[35]

And woe to the school board member who objects to being referred to as a "cis-sexual" when the federal bathroom police come knocking.

It is noteworthy that the Obama administration framed its bathroom pronouncements both in terms of danger of hate crimes against transvestites and coded references to political battles over illegal immigration. "Our guidance sends a clear message to transgender students across the country: here in America, you are safe, you are protected and you belong – just as you are," wrote Vanita Gupta, head of the Civil Rights Division of the Justice Department.[36]

Sometimes a bathroom battle is not just a bathroom battle.

Ms. Gupta's insinuation is clear, and the precedence for her insinuation is clear, too: anyone opposing any permutation of this vast societal transformation of children's bathrooms and teens' locker rooms are dangerous bigots and haters – potential hate criminals and potential perpetrators of identity-based violence. Such language was routinely used to justify the passage of hate crime laws in the 1990's. And when such accusations come from the very top of the federal Department of Justice, which itself empowered unelected leftist activist groups to determine what was and was not to be prosecuted as "hate," opponents to these directives have a great deal more to fear than merely the withholding of federal funds.

What is really at stake is the right to hold, or express, any view contrary to the increasingly radical leftist playbook, today on college campuses – tomorrow everywhere.

As has been amply documented by groups such as Accuracy in Academia, Campusreform.org, Dissident Prof, Truth Revolt, EAG Truth, FIRE, Minding the Campus, National Association of Scholars, Breitbart, and Project Veritas, college and university leaders have already de facto weakened or destroyed First Amendment rights throughout higher education, both in and outside classrooms. They have done so using euphemisms and excuses ranging from "restricting hate speech" to "providing safe spaces," to "encouraging diversity," and promoting "multiculturalism," "civility," or "sustainable campus climates."

Starting with identity-politics-suffused freshman orientation seminars that sometimes last a semester or longer, the intellectual indoctrination of students begins even before they set foot in any classroom to learn the real subjects they are ostensibly attending college to master.

Why do university and college administrators prioritize opinion "orientation" over academic subject matter itself? The answer lies in a powerful reciprocity between the federal agencies that qualify schools for federal student loans and research money and the armies of campus-based administrators whose sources of power lie in enforcing federal discrimination laws on the campuses themselves.

Mere tenured faculty members, who are themselves so overwhelmingly leftists that few even object to such federal interventions, are actually slipping down the totem poles of power on their own campuses. Good riddance, one might say. But what is replacing them is even worse: campus administrators working to limit free speech by bureaucratically redefining it as hate speech.

In order to understand why what happens on college campuses has implications for real courts, one need look no farther than the so-called campus-based "anti-rape" movement.

This movement, which has less to do with incarcerating real rapists than blaming all men for rape, offers a useful lesson in the dangers of legal reform movements nurtured and empowered on campuses and in law schools. The campus anti-rape movement has four power sources: student activists, campus women's centers and other campus administrative institutions, federal academic anti-discrimination laws, and law school and gender studies faculty who use their titles and research resources to push for vast transformations in state and federal laws.

The real danger of campus bureaucrats being empowered to behave with legal powers on campuses through federal academic discrimination laws is that these campus-based "legal" bureaucracies eventually burst the boundaries of the ivory tower and threaten to redefine the norms and priorities of the real legal system. Such redefinitions aim to impose the identity politics and political correctness priorities of campus life onto the real criminal justice system.

And this redefinition, as with all identity-politics based interventions in the legal system, inexorably moves our system of laws towards enforcing the subjective priorities of leftist ideology over the priority of actual law enforcement.

Identity politics policies and concurrent suppression of "hate speech" may be merely toxic on college campuses, but they have proven to be literally lethal in the real world of policing and crime, as the Rotherham child rape cases and the 2016 New Year's Eve mass public sexual assaults in Germany prove. None of these crimes would likely have occurred had the institutional suppression of "hate speech" criticizing Islamic rape culture and the administrative suppression of police investigations deemed politically incorrect not set them in motion.

Campus feminists' efforts to impose similar politically correct definitions of sexual assault are no longer confined to academia but are being lobbied for in state legislatures by armies of law and gender studies professors and students. Similar efforts on and off campuses are also now targeting the speech rights of research climate scientists who resist dominant views on global warming. And two decades ago, academicians, law professors and campus administrators united to lobby for hate crime laws that are now laying the groundwork for hate speech laws that will likely purge campuses of their remaining conservative faculty, further silence students, and turn conservative public figures into prosecutable hate criminals.

Behind all these efforts lies the federal law and education bureaucracies that provide activist administrators with broad powers to practice politics in the name of creating "inclusive and sustainable campus climates" – astonishingly ironic terms concealing administrative protocols dedicated to excluding people and suppressing free thought.

Also driving these efforts are the campus gender studies and environmental activism programs and law school clinics that provide scores of academic posts for manufacturing ever-more bizarre and punitive "research" and indoctrination about sex crimes, gender identities, climate research, hate crime law -- and now the legally permissible conduct and language addressing all of these subjects.

Set aside emotion and consider the impressive strategic deployment behind the seemingly overnight coup that resulted in transvestites' new rights to use any bathroom or locker room they choose. That movement emerged from gender studies programs and started on campuses just a few years ago. What's next? Campus politics, crazy as they may seem, and the research preoccupations of certain prominent academics offer clues for the next coordinated attack.

At this point, barring some interruption of the feedback loop between activist academicians, federal discrimination laws, and federal funding for academia, we can only expect more crazy-yet-effective social crusades and more individuals being targeted for silencing. And if the next movement, as I believe, will be to push for the passage of hate speech laws, all these social crusades will benefit from a powerful new tool to silence their political enemies, and the "gradschoolification of America" will spread even faster beyond college and university campuses.

Higher education is currently the main site of suppression of speech in America, but it may not remain so for long.

The Banning of Cliff Kincaid

The case of Cliff Kincaid being temporarily banned from speaking at SUNY New Paltz offers a window into a world of speech censorship that already exists throughout higher education – and exists despite tenured professors' long presumption that they are standard-bearers and exemplars of some type of special intellectual freedom: academic freedom.

The peculiar way the banning incident is being downplayed and even denied suggests that, publicly at least, SUNY New Paltz President Donald P. Christian does not wish to be identified as someone who would ban speakers from his campus. Some might interpret the re-inviting of Kincaid to the campus as a triumph of "academic freedom." But this is not true, as I will explain below. A closer look at President Christian's vigorous promotion of the Office of Compliance and Campus Climate suggests that re-inviting Kincaid to campus was more a way for him to quash a potential challenge to speech suppression than acknowledgement that freedom of expression ought to be defended on campuses – or anywhere else.

Tenured professors and especially law school professors love to pretend that they are special defenders of free speech and intellectual inquiry. But their utter failure to even recognize – let alone object to -- the sinister administrative fiats systematically outlawing free speech and inquiry in their own backyards represents an epic ethical failure, and an embarrassing intellectual and professional one as well.

Administrative bodies such as the SUNY New Paltz Office of Compliance and Campus Climate exist in direct opposition to notions of academic freedom that were codified for tenured faculty by the *1940 Statement on Principles for Academic Freedom and Tenure*. This code was written and passed by the American Association of University Professors as a professional credo applying to tenured professors and was subsequently upheld by various court decisions.

Despite widespread belief outside academia and self-indulgent belief within academia, the *Statement* never was actually a free speech right for everyone in the ordinary sense of the term but a job protection provided only to a narrow cohort of tenured faculty in the context of their jobs.

But even granting this narrow definition of academic freedom for some, the *Statement on Principles* has been systematically superseded by federal anti-discrimination laws and bureaucracies such as the Office of Compliance and Campus Climate, with nary a whimper from the tenured faculty who fancy themselves defenders of free speech.

On campuses, these federal discrimination protocols are used, with increasing creativity, to suppress speech and ideas in the name of "inclusion," "diversity," and "safe spaces." Such bureaucratic sprawl, mission creep, and the increasing empowerment of hate crime activists by federal agencies are effectively threatening even ordinary First Amendment speech rights and all academic freedom on campuses. Students and non-tenured faculty have already been silenced. Invited speakers are already vetted for "hate."

In a parallel movement, law professors such as Jeremy Waldron, campus branches of organizations such as the Southern Poverty Law Center, and other academicians (often in gender studies) are advancing arguments to justify expanding the use of the types of speech laws that already exist on college and university campuses beyond campus walls. The ultimate goal is to align U.S. hate crime laws with European and Canadian hate speech laws that now routinely punish and outlaw certain spoken and written political opinions as "hate." As with the transgender bathroom crusade, it is likely that demands to outlaw "hate speech" and criminalize individual "haters" will crescendo as the clock runs out on Obama's Departments of Justice and Education.

Administrative bodies such as SUNY New Paltz' Office of Compliance and Campus Climate, activist campus deans and presidents, and nonprofits granted special authority within certain federal agencies are on the front lines of these speech suppression crusades, and even if the next election leads to a Republican administration, these administrative entities and activist groups will not simply fold up shop and go away.

For this reason, the story of the way that Cliff Kincaid was disinvited from SUNY New Paltz is instructive. Kincaid's mere presence was described as a threat to both student safety and "campus climate." In essence, Kincaid wasn't merely banned from campus: he and his ideas were labeled as creating actual danger and harm. He was also blamed by the administration for the protests being fomented against him, thus tacitly endorsing the protesters' threats. This is rewarding the mob.

It is also sophisticated, late-stage censorship practiced by professional censors who know better than to merely ban a speaker for his views. The euphemisms of "campus climate" and "student safety" – euphemisms which now have their own leadership charts and office suites – have been the new normal on college campuses for some time now.

The purported threat Kincaid was said to pose to "campus climate" by his mere presence contains a warning for all of us: we are much further down the road of entirely banning mostly conservative ideas and speech, not only within our institutions of higher education but everywhere. This road will end with the suppression of all sorts of speech and ideas and ultimately people, not only in higher education but everywhere. And the source for this censorship lies in a hate crimes industry currently operating from a dual power base within the Federal Departments of Justice and Education.

The only response that will be effective to prevent the banning of speakers like Cliff Kincaid and even more serious threats to freedom of speech down the road is to target the hate crimes industry and its intentions to expand hate crime laws to pure speech acts. Academic freedom rules are of no use here. Academic freedom of thought, per se, never did really exist except for a select few. And even those few keep silent and watch over their shoulders fearfully these days. They might consider their complicity in the current state of affairs as they do so.

Surround and Destroy, But Quietly

On March 30, Cliff Kincaid was sitting in an airplane outside Washington D.C. waiting for the flight to take him to upstate New York, where he was scheduled to appear later in the day at the State University of New York (SUNY) New Paltz to debate liberal commentator and professor Jeff Cohen on the seemingly benign topic: "How the Media Can Sway Votes and Win Elections."

Sitting on the tarmac, Kincaid's phone rang. He was informed that he was not welcome on the SUNY New Paltz campus that day. The debate, he was told, had been cancelled because he was participating in it.

Kincaid now joins a growing list of conservative journalists and scholars banned or disinvited from college campuses in recent years. According to the Foundation for Individual Rights in Education (FIRE), formal dis-invitations, speakers withdrawing after threats, and so-called "heckler's vetoes" or mass disruptions of events are all on the rise.[37]

In addition to journalists and scholars being banned from campuses, increasing numbers of elected officials, both Democratic and Republican, are being disinvited from commencement ceremonies or subjected to such virulent protests that they opt to bow out. But in the narrow case of graduation ceremonies, the primary rationale in some of these cases at least seems plausible: that partisan politics would distract from the graduation ceremonies at the heart of such gatherings.

However, in the case of bans on individual public intellectuals, it is ideas themselves that are under fire, and it is almost exclusively conservatives being targeted. Liberals are occasionally banned too, but in the rare cases of liberal intellectuals being disinvited from campuses, the speaker involved is almost always someone who has been found guilty of plagiarism or who has committed serious crimes such as terrorism and murder. Examples include plagiarist Doris Kearns Goodwin, cop-killer Mumia Abu Jamal, and unrepentant terrorists Bill Ayers and Susan Rosenberg.

In contrast, for conservative intellectuals, merely holding conservative views is enough to unleash firestorms of criticism, outrage, and violent threats. David Horowitz, Michelle Malkin, Noni Darwish, Ann Coulter, Charles Murray, Ayaan Hirsi Ali, Roger Clegg, Dan Flynn, and Ben Shapiro are just a few of the conservative public intellectuals and journalists who have been driven from college campuses in recent years. Even student journalists report facing lesser forms of censorship: Eastern Connecticut State University student Jayson Veley, for example, writes that he published regularly in his student newspaper until he criticized the notion of "white privilege," in one op-ed. That was all it took: subsequently, all his op-ed submissions were rejected.[38]

Cliff Kincaid was at first surprised to discover that he had been targeted for exclusion from a debate about the media itself. "Jeff Cohen and I are friends," he told me. "We've done this debate about a dozen times before, particularly during presidential elections. We've never had a problem before." Indeed, their debate topic, "How the Media Can Sway Votes and Win Elections," could hardly sound more innocuous.

However, in recent years, Kincaid has been targeted by the Southern Poverty Law Center (SPLC), which has assembled a reserve fund, or endowment, of $301.8 million. Honest liberals understand and deplore the despicable tactics of the SPLC. Indeed, the SPLC has the unique distinction of having been discredited by just about everyone across the political spectrum, from arch-leftist Alexander Cockburn in *The Nation* to Ken Silverstein at *Harper's* magazine, to numerous conservatives including Matthew Vadum of Capital Research.[39] In 2014 the FBI finally stopped publicly partnering with the SPLC, but the group continues its campaign to profit from smearing conservatives with wild accusations of "hate."[40]

Despite the numerous exposés written about the SPLC, it remains enormously influential in both K – 12 academia and higher education thanks to its *Teaching Tolerance* publications, which are widely used by classroom teachers.

In reporting on the cancellation of the Cohen/Kincaid debate, the student newspaper at SUNY New Paltz,

The New Paltz Oracle, cited the Southern Poverty Law Center's accusations against Kincaid. But when the student journalists at the *Oracle* attempted to pin down the on-campus circumstances surrounding Kincaid's dis-inviting, they ran up against a wall of denials and bureaucratic doublespeak.[41]

As relayed by the *Oracle*, at some point after Kincaid had been invited to the campus to speak and the debate had been scheduled, his "controversial statements in the past about Muslims, climate change and homosexuals" were "discovered" by some unnamed person or persons and sparked a heated discussion on the faculty e-mail list. Parts of this discussion repeated in the student paper involved faculty members who encouraged the New Paltz community to attend the Kincaid/Cohen debate and confront Kincaid over views having nothing to do with the debate topic.

Sociology and women's studies professor Anne R. Roschelle, for example, stated that she was urging people to "ask critical questions and make your alternative voices heard." It seems clear from the context of her comments that Dr. Roschelle was not referring here to Kincaid's views on the media's role in election cycles, the subject of his talk, but to the political views he holds that are deemed unacceptable by the Southern Poverty Law Center.

Yet Dr. Roschelle claimed that she was not trying to disrupt the Kincaid/Cohen debate. "Given that I believe in free speech, I am not advocating he be uninvited or that people disrupt his talk," she said. It is difficult to imagine how both of her statements could be true: either she was encouraging students to interrupt a debate about the media's influence on election cycles or she was not.

Likewise, SUNY administrators quoted in the *Oracle* tried to deny that they were banning Kincaid because of his politics, and they even tried to deny that they were banning him at all: rather, they said, they were just cancelling an event that had somehow, mysteriously, through unnamed forces "got[ten] out of hand." They weren't banning Kincaid, they said, because of specific protest threats, but they also said they were cancelling it because the debate would likely be disrupted.

In a comment notable for its forceful denial of personal agency, Mike Patterson, director of the Office of Student Activities and Union Services, said that his office lacked "the structure and mechanisms in place" to "let there be a true, honest debate." He further euphemized: "The whole conversation wasn't going to be a debate but rather be a 'we don't like Kincaid' conversation ... We collectively agreed that the goal of the program got out of hand and went beyond what it needed to be."

SUNY New Paltz President Donald P. Christian further muddied the waters, issuing a mass e-mail simultaneously praising the Office of Student Activities for hosting the debate while praising the faculty for vigilantly unearthing the troubling details of Kincaid's background that cancelled the debate.

And so in the aftermath of the banning of Cliff Kincaid, three professional academicians said as little as possible in order to justify saying nothing out loud about what they were actually doing: reacting hysterically because someone who failed to entirely conform with the intellectual diktat had nearly breached the walls of their taxpayer-funded citadel to modestly debate the role of the media in presidential elections for upwards of two hours before climbing back into an airplane and flying home again.

The silver lining here may be that the young reporters at the *Oracle* now have an object lesson in political reporting with which to work as they disentangle real timelines and facts from the vague and contradictory record of official demurrals to date.[42]

Academia and Dictatorships

One line of questioning these student journalists might explore is their own institution's highly touted relationship with Cuba, a dictatorship where journalists are still imprisoned for criticizing government officials. Regarding who and who is not politically acceptable to campus officials, questions might also be raised about the financially profitable relationships that universities throughout the United States, and in New York State and the SUNY system in particular, maintain with China and Middle Eastern Islamic states where journalists and bloggers (such as they exist) are routinely imprisoned, tortured and murdered; where there is no free press; where slavery still exists, and where women and homosexuals are murdered with impunity for violating the extreme restrictions placed on every aspect of their lives.

For example, both Georgetown and Harvard Universities have received millions from Saudi Prince Alwaleed bin Talal of the repressive Saudi hierarchy. As reported by the Investigative Project on Terrorism: "[i]n December 2005, Harvard announced that Alwaleed had given $20 million to establish an Islamic Studies Program and Georgetown University announced he had contributed $20 million for the Prince Alwaleed Bin-Talal Center for Muslim-Christian Understanding headed by John Esposito."[43] Yale University also actively lobbies for Alwaleed's favors and cash.

The *New York Post* uncovered Iranian government money being funneled to Rutgers and Columbia Universities through Alavi Foundation, described as a front group for Mahmoud Ahmadinejad, the Iranian dictator and Holocaust denier:

> Anti-Israel, pro-Iran university professors are being funded by a shadowy multimillion-dollar Islamic charity based in Manhattan that the feds charge is an illegal front for the repressive Iranian regime.

The deep-pocketed Alavi Foundation has aggressively given away hundreds of thousands of dollars to Columbia University and Rutgers University for Middle Eastern and Persian studies programs that employ professors sympathetic to the Iranian dictatorship.

"We found evidence that the government of Iran really controlled everything about the foundation," said Adam Kaufmann, investigations chief at the Manhattan District Attorney's Office.

Federal law-enforcement authorities are in the midst of seizing up to $650 million in assets from the Alavi Foundation, which they charge funnels money to Iran-supported Islamic schools in the United States and to a syndicate of Iranian spies based in Europe.[44]

SUNY New Paltz journalism students might also consider the redirection of resources and slots for American college students to the children of the ruling classes in Communist China. Not only does China imprison and torture journalists: the admission of hundreds of thousands of foreign students from China is beginning to severely impact admission of American students to schools that are subsidized by their own parents' tax dollars. As Phyllis Schlafly recently reported:

> The numbers of Chinese and other foreign students who go to college in the U.S. is truly mind-boggling.
>
> The University of Illinois has 5,000 Chinese students on its Champaign-Urbana campus, compared with less than 100 a decade ago. Students from the People's Republic of China made up a tenth of last year's freshman class.
>
> California . . . admit[s] huge numbers of students from mainland China, including 1,200 at UC Berkeley (up from 47 a decade ago) and 2,200 at UC San Diego (up from 70). Of the nearly 1 million people living in the United States on F-1 student visas, about 360,000 are from China.[45]

How do journalism programs and university presidents justify banning a Cliff Kincaid while simultaneously pandering to and accepting money from terrorist front groups, dictators, and their apologists -- people who literally murder or once murdered journalists? The answer is they don't justify it. They let political correctness and identity politics do the work of papering over their pandering to repressive Islamic regimes, and they let historical ignorance and higher education's long love affair with communist dictatorships do the work of obscuring their own ironic celebration of American journalists who spied for mass murderers like Joseph Stalin.

Underlying this cynicism is a particularly powerful strain of moral blindness regarding the century-long toll on free speech and freedom of expression by communists. In fact, the story of academia's treatment of Cliff Kincaid versus its treatment of his debate partner Jeff Cohen – Kincaid banned from campus and Cohen rewarded professionally for honoring a journalist who abetted dictators who killed journalists – illuminates the practically incredible double standard that rules higher education.

Cliff Kincaid is the longtime Director of the AIM Center for Investigative Journalism at the conservative media watchdog group Accuracy in Media. He also runs America's Survival, a non-profit educational organization that opposes American involvement in the United Nations, seeks justice for murdered police and other forgotten victims of leftist and communist violence, investigates politicians' ties to communism, and documents the flow of money from figures such as billionaire hedge fund operator George Soros to left-wing radicals in the media, academia, and other nonprofits.

Kincaid's debating partner, Jeff Cohen, is also a media critic, writing, however, from the Left instead of the Right and from inside academia instead of outside it. Cohen is the founder of FAIR, a progressive media watchdog group. He is co-founder of the "media action" group RootsAction.org and an Associate Journalism Professor and director of the Park Center for Independent Media at Ithaca College.

Cohen's activism and teaching both take place at Ithaca College, a private college that nonetheless receives federal assistance (as do virtually all private colleges) through federally guaranteed student loan programs and other public subsidies. An unwitting public, including both New York State and federal taxpayers, therefore underwrites his activism.

The banning of Cliff Kincaid from merely speaking at a college about election-time media, on the grounds that elsewhere he holds "extremist" views (as categorized by the Southern Poverty Law Center) offers an object lesson in the moral priorities of academicians who deem such views more relevant that the actual imprisonment and murder of journalists by the communist regimes of Stalin-era and present-day Cuba.

For the faculty and administrators at SUNY New Paltz who eagerly denounced Kincaid are also currently eagerly embracing the Castro regime and arranging exchange programs with Cuba despite the fact that journalists there still languish in prisons, and speaking ill of Fidel Castro still earns a reporter or blogger a prison term. Despite the ongoing oppression of journalists and ordinary citizens in Cuba, SUNY New Paltz eagerly announced that a dean for its Center of International Programs and its vice president for Enrollment Management recently joined a select delegation to Cuba and that the U.S. Department of Treasury has granted the school permission to move forward with faculty and student exchanges.[46]

As one of only twelve U.S. colleges and universities selected to develop exchange programs with Cuba through this prestigious program, one might ask whether Cuba's horrendous treatment of journalists and suppression of a free press is of any concern to SUNY New Paltz President Donald P. Christian or the faculty of the school's Digital Media and Journalism Program.

President Christian's only published comment on the Cuba-New Paltz program was to give it a "shout out" in one of his public commentaries. No faculty member in the school's Department of Digital Media and Journalism has gone on record criticizing Cuba's oppression of journalists or suppression of free speech by citizens.

Kincaid's debate partner, Professor Jeff Cohen, similarly institutionalizes this ethical double standard at nearby Ithaca College, where his Park Center for Independent Media administers a prize named for a Stalinist spy who assisted a regime that murdered millions of civilians, including journalists.

Neither the Izzy Award nor its namesake, Soviet spy I.F. Stone, is controversial in academic circles. Instead, journalism professors revere Stone. However, Harvey Klehr, John Earl Haynes, and Alexander Valliliev documented that Stone's codename was "Pancake" and he was recruited by the Soviet KGB to assist Soviet intelligence. He was an agent of influence who functioned as a spy as well, including such tasks as "talent spotting, acting as a courier by relaying information to other agents, and providing private journalistic tidbits and data the KGB found interesting." [47] However, it also appears that Stone had an on-again, off-again relationship with the KGB.

I.F. Stone chose to work on behalf of a genocidal dictator who shut down all independent media in his own country and suppressed all free speech and free scholarship. In the name of communism, for more than a century and continuing today, Stalin and his peers in other communist nations including China and Cuba have effectively cut hundreds of millions of people off from intellectual freedom and freedom of speech, from non-state sanctioned history and literature, and from accurate information about their own governments.

A journalism award in a communist's honor is an intellectual contradiction so severe that it could only survive in the hallucinatory incoherence that is higher education.

Recipients of Ithaca College's Izzy Awards include such committed leftists as Glenn Greenwald, who published classified information on behalf of former National Security Agency (NSA) analyst Edward Snowden, and Amy Goodman, who may be best known for interviewing people like Bill Ayers and Bernardine Dohrn in their "first joint broadcast interview" after the 2008 presidential election. Goodman, co-host of Democracy Now!, is so far to the left that she ran a special program honoring Castro collaborator Che Guevara. Her co-host, Juan Gonzalez, was a member of Students for a Democratic Society, which spawned the terrorist Weather Underground.

None of these activities -- from treasonously spying for an enemy government while it committed mass murder of its citizens and killed its own journalists, to threatening to release illegally obtained classified data that would similarly endanger Americans' lives -- raises eyebrows among the leftist cognoscenti. In fact, in academia, with its odd fusion of frivolity and deadly serious deployment of cultural power, doing such things is considered merely edgy. It gets one showered with awards, prizes, and prestigious academic posts.

"Izzy" Stone himself justified colluding with dictators who imprisoned and murdered journalists and millions of other on the grounds that he had a right to do so as a member of the media in a free capitalist society – and never mind that he was seeking to overthrow that free society to turn it into another speech-repressive communist dictatorship.

I mention the I.F. Stone awards here at length to drive home the point that colleges and universities have, since the 1950's onward, prided themselves as being unique and necessary sanctuaries for even the most extreme and indefensible ideas and speech – so long as it was the right flavor of extreme and indefensible ideas and speech.

Stone's dream of overthrowing the U.S. government and his communist master vision of eliminating all private property understandably limited his appeal outside the ivory tower. He sought and found fame largely among academicians after ordinary audiences rejected his ideas. And it is a curiosity worth considering that he continues to be celebrated within academia even as evidence mounted affirming his involvement in the murderous international secret spy network Stalin nurtured, even though he publicly disavowed Stalin himself.

If anything, recent revelations confirming Stone's spying for Russia have only enhanced his reputation in academic circles. Such are the contours of academia's unique delineation of what is and is not "free speech": a journalist who abetted a dictator who murdered thousands of journalists and crushed free speech throughout half the world for half a century only grows in stature as a hero of free speech – in the eyes of academicians – as the evidence of his culpability in suppressing free speech grows.

'See?' the elite journalism professors seem to be saying, 'we are so committed to the idea of free speech for journalists and for us that even a journalist who spent his life justifying a regime that killed other journalists and suppressed speech for hundreds of millions is to be celebrated.'

Of course, the academicians who celebrate I.F. Stone don't really say such things, and they don't really see their own behavior this way. Stone and his peers are celebrated at Ithaca College, at Columbia University's prestigious journalism school, and in other journalism schools throughout the country not because he or they represent "free speech" or "academic freedom" but because he and they stand for empowering a particular politics with a particular history, be it "socialism," "communism," anti-capitalism," and their younger siblings "progressivism," "multiculturalism," "identity politics," or the new academic euphemism for all of these themes: "sustainability." Never mind that these things, too, are merely suppression of free speech under increasingly Orwellian titles.

There are intellectual and historical arguments that may be made about the evolution of I.F. Stone's commitment to Stalin and more specifically his henchmen, or what he knew when about the murder and imprisonment of millions in Russia or the starvation of millions in Ukraine, or his intentions for the United States after the dreamed-of communist overthrow of representational democracy that animated his life's labor. But it would be disingenuous to pretend that awards such as the "Izzys" have anything to do with permitting, let alone encouraging intellectual inquiries into that history or any other.

In academia, historical inquiry and debate about public figures like I.F. Stone and ideologies like communism are a firmly closed book. Increasingly, any such deviation from the official version of the heroes and villains of liberty and history are alien to the purpose of academic institutions themselves.

A debate between Cliff Kincaid and Jeff Cohen -- even one that deteriorated into an attack on Kincaid -- would likely have offered the students at SUNY New Paltz at least the opportunity to think about the difference between the officially sanctioned version of journalism history represented by things such as "Izzy" awards granted by tenured professors running well-funded Centers for Independent Media from within academia versus the sort of independent media practiced by anti-communist journalists like Cliff Kincaid who are now not even welcome to set foot on campus to present their views.

So, no matter how many journalistic courage awards are handed out at Ithaca's Park Center, or the Poynter Institute, or the Columbia Journalism School, these awards should not be interpreted as proof that freedom of expression actually exists at those places. In fact, as growing numbers of students and their parents are finally noticing, American college and university campuses rank among the least intellectually free places in our nation.

And speaking of suppression of thought and speech on campus, to date, not one faculty member has spoken out publicly against banning Kincaid from campus, unless one ironically counts the demurrals of those such as Dr. Roschelle who claimed to be criticizing his presence without actually calling for his absence. There may be professors who objected to the dis-invitation from the safety of faculty comment threads, but nobody took a public stand. Not even one tenured professor publicly objected to the banning of someone who holds conservative views on their own campus. This speaks volumes about the absolute power of a leftist political monoculture that is increasingly capable of threatening even tenured professors, now that they are done silencing the rest of us.

Frivolity and Power

College campuses are the ground zero of an intellectual twilight setting over America. A curious characteristic of this twilight – and one that separates them from other intellectual twilights in other countries where academics themselves were actually risking their lives fighting for free speech -- is the fusion of intellectual frivolity with cultural power. Over the span of merely fifty years, the mission of higher education (in the humanities, at least) as the ticket both to a comfortable middle-class life and "the life of the mind" for many tens of millions of people has taken a back seat to the politics and hobbies of professors who justify their lack of intellectual seriousness with a hoary, Bernie Sanders-like constellation of narrow, far-left activism.

As this radically left-wing political monoculture insinuates itself deeper into the day-to-day operations of colleges and universities, dissenting faculty, students and employees alike know that self-censorship is the safest path to avoiding conflict with three powerful forces that exist on every campus:

- Roving bands of activist students who react with protests, hysteria (in the Freudian sense), manifestos, sit-ins, and worse whenever they perceive a whiff of resistance to their whims and desires.

- Activist professors, often operating out of "studies" programs and teaching freshmen survey courses, whose primary area of weirdly narcissistic study is their own identity and/or sexual preferences.

- A cowed, complicit, or activist administration.

Scratch the surface of any humanities, social sciences, or law school department in any school in America and one will find the same themes relentlessly and loudly declaimed:

- Blacks, Hispanics, illegal immigrants, Native Americans and other mostly brown-skinned minorities are subject to absolute and endless oppression at the hands of whites and also the more free-floating idea of "white privilege."

- Oppressed, too, are (liberal) women, gays, lesbians, transvestites, the transgendered, and an ever-growing list of "other identified" sexual minorities who reject "gender-binaries," "cis-sexuality," and all persons who fail to continuously fine-tune their reactions to the ever-evolving sea of sexual re-identification occurring around them.

- Capitalism in all its permutations is evil, as is oil (especially fracking), banking (especially student loans), Republicans, patriotism, Joseph McCarthy, Christianity and Judaism (except the Unitarian strains), suburbs, police, automobiles (though neither planes nor trains), change-resistant lower-class white Americans, and, of course, their native lingua franca: "hate speech."

- Criminals are good; communist Cuba is good; communism in general would be good if only it could be practiced "freely"; third-world despots are at the bare minimum misunderstood, if not well intentioned, or even heroic, as are Islamic terrorists, the IRA, Ché Guevara, the Weathermen, the Black Panthers, the Red Army, Mao Zedong, and Fidel Castro.

While a Cliff Kincaid debating media coverage during a presidential election cycle is perceived as an immediate threat and provokes the deepest outrage and administrative action from the highest levels, consider the following speakers who are considered non-controversial. Consider that attracting speakers of this academic caliber are notable accomplishments of SUNY New Paltz, an otherwise financially modest school. Scarce money is spent on such topics, even as students face tuitions increases and march on Albany to complain about them (they might consider protesting closer to home):

> On April 3, WGSS [Women's, Gender & Sexuality Studies Program] hosted Professor Jane Ward (Women's Studies, University of California, Riverside) for our third biennial

Queer Studies Lecture. Addressing an over-capacity room of students, faculty, staff and community members, Ward's talk – "Not Gay: Whiteness, Masculinity, and the Remaking of Homosexual Sex" – drew on themes from her forthcoming book (NYU Press)...

Ward argued that straight white men leverage their experiences of homosexual sex to bolster their own heterosexuality and masculinity. She suggested that instead of thinking of them as "closeted gays," we might use their example to think about heterosexuality in new ways—not as the opposite or absence of homosexuality, but as its own unique mode of engaging homosexual sex, a mode characterized by pretense, disidentification [sic], and racialized heteronormative[sic] investments. Ward's lively and provocative talk continued to be discussed – in classrooms, university hallways, and on social media – for many days following her visit. We look forward to an equally thought-provoking Queer Studies Lecture in 2016![48]

The WSGG Department also features one Dr. Jessica N. Pabón, an Assistant Professor of Women's, Gender, and Sexuality Studies. Dr. Pabón teaches "feminist performance aesthetics, Hip Hop culture, latina/o studies, identity and community in lgbtq and queer theory, subcultural performance, transnational feminisms, and US feminist of color theory."[49]

Here is the description of her latest "book project":

> *Graffiti Grrlz: Performing Feminism in the Hip Hop Diaspora* contributes a pivotal intervention to Hip Hop cultural studies grounded in Queer, Feminist, and Performance Studies. *Graffiti Grrlz* is an interdisciplinary ethnography analyzing over a decade of physical and digital research with over 75 female-identified graffiti artists from 17 countries. Arguing that graffiti subculture is a transnational arts movement rooted in US-based AfroCaribbean diasporic sensibilities, she examines the aesthetic, social, and political strategies of resistance (such as performing feminist masculinity, building affective community, and using digital media) employed to navigate the material effects of being female-bodied in a male-dominated subculture.[50]

Pabon spent a year in Abu Dubai under the auspices of New York University, not studying the treatment of women or male slave labor there but documenting hip-hop graffiti for her TED talks.[51] The NYU Abu Dhabi Annual Research Conference 2014 features her contribution to the program: "Performing Women: 'All-Female Jams' in Beat boxing, Breakdancing, and Graffiti Writing"[52] There is no mention anywhere in her work of any negative impression of Abu Dhabi as an autocratic, misogynistic slave state.

And of course, there would not be. One does not get ahead in one's research on feminist beat boxing, Grrlz graffiti, white lady breakdancing, diaspora sensibility, and certainly not Queer Performance Studies by biting the hands of one's funders even if they are Islamic gender oppressors and you are a professor of Women's Gender & Sexuality Studies.

The spectacle of one professor of gender studies doing graffiti research in Dubai; another writing about food allergies as a rights issue and imagining she is documenting feminist resistance in Afghanistan while playing tourist with other self-indulgent academicians;[53] of the SUNY campuses collecting little bottles of shampoo for rape victims while their law departments work to spring real rapists, and college presidents tumbling over each other to be the first to take Anthony Bourdain-style Potemkin Village tours of Cuba to prove their more-authentic leftist credentials to other leftists is the frivolous side of the Janus face of academia today.

On the other side, these same activities reveal something far less amusing in that it is used in service to a deeply toxic anti-Americanism and a naivety about totalitarianism that should have been at least modestly revaluated in the last half century.

The silly professor breakdancing in Dubai thinks she is "opening vistas." She isn't. She's covering for an autocratic, misogynistic slave state -- on fellowship by said slave state, of course. The professors in Cuba think they're celebrating freedom. They're not.

They're helping propagandize the continuing repression of others while falling for the sort of Potemkin Village nonsense about which they ought to have learned something – anything – because after all, they are supposed to be people who learn things.

Behind these infantilized acts of "studying" Grrlz graffiti, Brony scholarship (a real thing[54]), Afghani women's landay poetry readings, by non-Afghani women, in Boston coffee shops (*My Nabi was shot down by a drone. May God destroy your sons, America, you murdered my own*),[55] the Cuban cigars proudly displayed at the department holiday party, the little bottles of used shampoo sanctimoniously gathered for rape victims who do not need used shampoo, nor anti-male campus agitprop, but access to real courts, lies an almost limitless, unthinking rage at America and at people who do not think like them and look like them and believe what they believe, down to the last Brony ponytail and the new gender identity they invented last week.

Rage, frivolity, and activism have so thoroughly supplanted scholarship (in the humanities) in America that the resulting cognitive dissonance requires some external authority to continue binding the status quo. That this authority is coming in the form of Compliance and Campus Climate Committees and witch hunts by federal agencies in coordination with the Southern Poverty Law Center should surprise no-one who has studied the ways by which freedom was stripped from citizens and replaced with propaganda and speech control in countries that transformed into socialist or communist or otherwise totalitarian states. But for others, apparently, that sort of thing isn't taught in schools anymore.

From "Safe Spaces" to "Campus Climate"

In banning Cliff Kincaid from the SUNY New Paltz campus, President Christian and the specific administrators and professors were engaging in a highly stylized farce, one that plays out daily on campuses throughout the United States. Where once students demanded the "right" to "free speech" no matter how offensive or inane (or frequently, both), they now demand something that seems, on the surface at least, to be the opposite: the right to "safe spaces" where they might be protected from speech and ideas deemed so threatening that undergraduates and other living things must be physically sheltered from them, lest mere contact with a sign reading "Men's Room" or the words "Trump '16" chalked on a sidewalk cause permanent harm.

Campus "safe spaces" are, in one sense, merely the latest iteration of a long cascade of separationist perks, housing, academic departments, and special programming demanded by and provided to various radicals who manage to intimidate or guilt-trip their way to receiving the budget line-items they desire. But the satisfaction of separatism has its limits, both for the students who have already received every special perk and precondition they demanded and still don't feel satisfied, and the administrators whose salaries and fiefdoms literally depend on ongoing campus crises and oppressions and discriminations and manufactured "hate incidents."

For both parties, and also for the federal agencies upstream from them, the invention of "safe space" culture has been an ideological godsend. Claims of being rendered "unsafe" or "triggered" eliminate the need for actual acts of violence or discrimination to take place (rare or imaginary as they were to begin with).

The apparatus of the safe space movement began with the creation of women's centers on campuses – woman-only sites heavy with scented candles, yoga lunches, speculum self-examination empowerment circles (don't ask), moldering crates of Take Back the Night t-shirts and other detritus of second-wave feminism so stereotypical that even hipsters make fun of it on popular cable television shows.[56]

The hate crimes industry used gay student Tyler Clementi's suicide to expand the idea of safe spaces into a virtue signaling opt-in program involving stickers placed on the doors of campus faculty and administrators who chose to certify their offices as official "safe spaces" for presumably threatened gay and lesbian students – a sort of reverse pink triangle – and also an insinuation that gays and lesbians are so specially emotionally or physically threatened that they literally need a certified space to which to retreat.

Of course, it is the professors and administrators who choose to not blazon their doors with safe space agitprop that are the real targets of such campaigns. By refusing to participate, they are placed, by default, in the position of being identified as not caring about the safety of endangered gay and lesbian lives, just as opponents of hate crime laws are routinely accused of approving of the violent murders of minorities and even the historical oppression of blacks.

The safe space movement took the separationist enclaves of feminist women's spaces and expanded them to encompass entire campuses by dividing offices, departments, and other physical spaces into the designation "safe" or "unsafe." Now the movement has expanded again to encompass curriculum, books, speakers, classrooms and entire disciplines. Students demand "trigger warnings" so they may exclude themselves from "traumatic" subjects, and many faculty members now routinely incorporate such warnings in their syllabi. Academic guest speakers and even entertainment figures like comedians have been hit with warnings or banned entirely for employing "triggering" speech or broaching "triggering" subjects, a list that grows larger every passing semester.

It was in this environment that Cliff Kincaid was deemed "unsafe" to appear on the SUNY New Paltz campus, and it is evidence of the recent metastasizing of this therapeutically framed proto-fascist speech control that Kincaid has been performing this debate with Jeff Cohen for years with no problems up until now.

It is also evidence of the institutionalizing of this sort of activism through administrative bodies empowered by the federal government. At SUNY New Paltz, either someone with no sense of humor or a very good Orwellian one has named the administrative body tasked with enforcing federal discrimination laws or campus diversity demands the office of Compliance and Campus Climate (surely, any acronymic similarity to the Council of Conservative Citizens was merely coincidental).

The SUNY CCC was created, as many such bodies are, in the wake of a spate of alleged hate crimes that were, as such things usually are, vigilantly investigated before disappearing into the ether after police either found no offenders or found minority students and/or leftist ones to be the culprits, at which point all such investigations disappear into official wormholes, never to emerge again.[57]

Nevertheless, President Christian took advantage of the utterly ridiculous spate of questionable hate crimes (which involved a piece of tape over a water fountain and a paper cutout of a hand with bad words written on it and the middle finger raised) to issue forth a tidal wave of proclamations denouncing "hatred" and creating a new office – the CCC – to concretely bureaucratize the persistence of his vigilance to keep the idea alive that the campus over which he presided was a hotbed of Klan-like activities that he would valiantly battle. In introducing the creation of the CCC, Christian wrote:

> As we learned in the aftermath of the posting of racially offensive material on campus in

fall 2011, even communities such as New Paltz that are known for their diversity must address issues of race and racial equity – and other dimensions of diversity, equity, and inclusiveness. The forum, "Can We Talk About It," held in November 2011 was the first step in an effort to heal the wounds opened by that incident, and pointed out the need for continued examination and discussion of these important topics on our campus and in our society. The student-planned and –led TRANSactions event held in spring 2012, programs being planned by the Student Association during spring 2013, and discussion of the experiences of LGBTQ students and employees are continuing those conversations. The new Office of Compliance and Campus Climate and the Executive Director will play a leadership role in this work.[58]

This executive director, Tanheda Pacheco Dunn, is officially tasked with serving as the point person enforcing federal discrimination directives, but she is also granted broad latitude in participating in hiring decisions and "training" students and employees who presumably fail to conform to federal and institutional standards regarding diversity:

> Pacheco Dunn is responsible for monitoring the college's compliance with all applicable laws, regulations, policies, and procedures as they apply to: Title IX provisions that deal

with sexual assault, sexual harassment, and hostile workplace issues; affirmative action; and New York State ethics legislation. This includes resolving complaints, making policy recommendations, designing and facilitating training for students and employees (with support from Student Affairs and Human Resources respectively), and coordinating interdepartmental efforts to comply with these employment legislations.

Additional duties include developing and administering the college's affirmative action plan; determining outcomes of employee accommodation requests; participation in the college's various employee search processes and serving as the point of contact on relevant compliance questions from state, federal or other regulatory agencies.[59]

President Christian was far more fulsome in his description of his vision for the CCC. He wrote of creating "opportunities for conversation so we may grow in our commitment to respect, equity and inclusion." Those opportunities, he wrote, would include "educational training and programming on equity and inclusiveness."

Also, "[t]he Office of Compliance and Campus Climate will work with student leaders to identify opportunities for productive inquiry that models respectful behavior and engagement, helping to prepare them for responsible citizenship beyond the university."

And: "[i]n my inaugural address, I outlined the following as a critical goal for the New Paltz campus: create a campus climate that is increasingly inclusive and equitable. That goal underscores our mission of educating all members of the College to live in and contribute to a diverse global society."[60]

Invented out of a surely faked racial incident, the office of Compliance and Campus Climate sends a pointed message from President Christian to SUNY New Paltz students that any deviation from or even lack of enthusiasm for a set of approved views on diversity, affirmative action, inclusiveness, and something called "respectful behavior" "modeled" by the diversity enforcers may result in "educational training on equity and inclusiveness."

In 2013, the SUNY New Paltz LGBTQ Task Force of the Campus Climate administration issued a 30-page report that reveals the extent to which the CCC plans to control every aspect of the "campus climate" inside and outside of classrooms.[61]

The report itself is worthy of its own study, but to summarize, it begins with demands for a plethora of new resources and campus-wide dictates including funding lines, "Inclusive Name Use," "Gender Inclusive Housing," dedicated administrators, course offerings, requirements to inquire and conform to gender pronouns in all cases, from application materials, to student aid, to student I.D., and faculty addressing students. It also recommends mandating training and interventions for all students and faculty – demands if, which met, would literally require SUNY New Paltz and all students attending there to essentially minor in LGBT issues, overseen by LGBT activists and administrators – all of which would be subsidized by the students and taxpayers of New York State. Doubtlessly, President Christian will implement any and every aspect of the Task Force that the students and taxpayers can possibly find a way to subsidize.

That this "Climate Control" agency is combined with the bureaucracy dedicated to enforcing "Compliance" with federal administrative discrimination and diversity protocols is a threat in a velvet glove.

But that is not the worst of it. Universities in America are already using the safe spaces and Climate Control-style initiatives to ban public speakers and monitor the content of what is taught in classrooms.

The situation is far worse in countries that lack the free speech protections Americans enjoy. No less a far-left media source as *The Guardian* actually spoke out recently about the implications of these measures for restricting free speech – even free feminist speech. The article is worth reading not only because a leftist publication views these trends as a problem, but because it offers a sense of what will happen rapidly here is hate speech laws such as those in Britain are achieved in America, as American academicians and college presidents are working to coordinate now:

> [T]he [banning of comedian] Smurthwaite ... reveals something troubling about the culture on Britain's campuses. Whatever the precise reasons for the cancellation, the feminist society took a vote to picket someone because of a policy position unrelated to the content of the show itself. This is not like the antifascist "no platform" campaign of the 1980s and 90s. It is much broader and more nebulous. The potential for offence is trumping the right to free speech.

The row comes amid a growing sense of crisis around debate in British universities. In recent months, Oxford University cancelled a debate on abortion because protesters objected to the fact it was being held between two men; the Cambridge Union was asked (but refused) to withdraw its speaking invitation to Germaine Greer because of her views on transgender issues; officials at London Southbank took down a "flying spaghetti monster" poster because it might cause religious offence; UCL banned the Nietzsche Club after it put up posters saying "equality is a false God", and Dundee banned the Society for the Protection of Unborn Children from their freshers' fair. The Sun is banned on dozens of campuses because of Page 3. Robin Thicke's Blurred Lines song has also been banned by many student unions.

There are two ways of looking at the challenges to free speech on college campuses – quantitative and qualitative – and it's getting worse on both counts," says Joanna Williams of Kent University's Enhancement of Learning and Teaching unit, who has written extensively about politics on campus. "Censorship powers are being used more often and against a wider variety of targets." [62]

The abortion debate was cancelled at Christ Church College of Oxford University, a combined church and academic institution and alma mater to John Locke, Robert Hooke, John Wesley, Robert Peel, William Gladstone, and W.H. Auden. Administers bowed to student pressure to cancel the debate because feminists protested the mere concept of "cis-men" debating the sanctity of life.[63] Any doubts that so-called "hate speech" laws will not lead to official second-class status (or worse) for men, heterosexuals, pro-life advocates, and anyone holding conservative views should look to the controversies currently roiling British university campuses.

The speed with which such laws delegate certain classes of people to second-class citizenship, and then prosecutable as literal thought criminals, has been demonstrated in one western nation after another. Still, hate crime activists; their political enablers (Democrats, but also Republicans who refuse to take a stand against such laws); and college and university presidents such as Donald P. Christian push forward with this crusade.

In the 1990's, hate crime laws were passed in Congress and in most states in America with the explicit promise that these laws would never impose on First Amendment rights by criminalizing "mere speech." It is a tribute to our powerful tradition of defending free speech that this assertion was given great weight at the time while other, seeming more contradictory definitional problems were brushed over in haste, especially by the Congressional and Senatorial committees hearing arguments for or against the passage of federal hate crime laws.

For example, the sticky wicket of "counting" serial rape/murder as hate received but a few nervous comments from then-president Bill Clinton, who argued against their inclusion as hate crimes even though they met every definition of so-called hate (victims randomly selected because of their identity; attacked in ways to specifically humiliate that identity; using extreme violence, and spreading fear among other members of the class of people who shared the identity "potential female victim of rape and murder" with the actual murdered-and-raped women).

Before a nationally-broadcast conference in 1997, Clinton hemmed and hawed a bit at questions about counting or not counting such women before muttering that there were just too many of them to be counted -- that is, too many raped and murdered women to call them hate crime victims because then most hate crime victims would be women and a heck of a lot of the offenders would be black men, and that wasn't the point of this whole thing anyway, right?

Meanwhile, it was uncontroversial that uttering a slur while carjacking someone not only could but should be counted as a hate crime.

To truly understand hate crime laws as they exist in reality (or enforcement, whichever term one prefers), it has to first be understood that all hate crime laws are predicated almost exclusively on speech to begin with, and not all speech but some speech directed at not all victims but only some of them, the ones with the best lobbies and a seat at the right tables.

Yet speech alone still supersedes other evidence contradicting the existence of "hate crime" when the case is deemed too valuable to the activists. Speech alone is evidence that the most famous gay hate crime of all time, the murder of Matthew Shepard, was a gay hate crime and not primarily the consequence of Shepard leaving a nightclub to score meth and party with criminally violent men from whom he met a violent end (as did the mother of one of Shepard's killers, under nearly identical circumstances).

The meth and violent offender aspects of Shepard's murder were and are culturally and politically irrelevant: it was only the speech that counted and the fact that it was directed against him.

Academic Crusade for Hate Speech Laws

Pure speech bias crime has been "not counted" in the U.S. for twenty years now, in contrast to Canada and Britain and France because the First Amendment dictates against it.

But with the passage of President Obama's Matthew Shepherd and James Byrd Jr. Hate Crimes Act of 2009, curiously, hate speech became an issue again. This is not explicit in the law – but nothing is explicit in these laws – however, the 2009 law did two things to get us to where we are today, which is several steps closer to pure hate speech convictions. First, it added the category of anti-homosexual hate crime to the federal roster, opening the door to prosecuting ministers and many observant religious people. It simultaneously expanded federal powers to enter into state hate crime cases dramatically, thus bringing the federal apparatus to bear.

The Shepherd/Byrd Act of 2009 rejuvenated the fight for pure hate speech laws in America modeled on British, Canadian and European models. The other impetus was the Obama administration's emphasis on anti-Muslim hate speech incidents. The publication of Jeremy Waldron's 2012 book, *The Harm in Hate Speech*, has reignited a law-school based campaign to lobby for expanding existing hate crime laws to include pure speech acts. Waldron, a professor at both New York University School of Law and an endowed professor of Social and Political Theory at All Souls College, University of Oxford, has received admittedly mixed reviews for even those who admire his book, including Stanley Fish and retired Supreme Court Justice John Paul Stevens.

But let me venture a prediction here, based on three points:

First, hate crime laws are already enforced in ways that are so subjective and so dominated by activist groups officially empowered by the Department of Justice to determine both definitions and prosecutions of hate that we are already manipulating these laws in ways that only punish speech.

Second, Supreme Court Justice Elena Kagan, who worked under Eric Holder to help Bill Clinton keep women from being counted as hate crime victims, is one of the people Waldron thanks for helping shape the book.

Third, the fanfare accompanying Waldron's book and its alignment with policies already being practiced to radically suppress free speech on college campuses suggests a movement within academia to make hate speech laws the capstone of the Obama administration's "transformation" of America.

We would be unwise to fail to explore this possibility further.

Appendices

- Appendix A: Statement of President Donald P. Christian on the Office of Compliance and Campus Climate:

Mission Statement

The office of the Executive Director for Compliance and Campus Climate is charged with oversight of a variety of mandates that impact the ways in which the institution engages with its constituents. To that end, this office will work collaboratively and proactively to reach across functional silos and to act and serve as a resource for the community. Beyond compliance with laws and policy, this office is committed to enhance a community that demands excellence and integrity, values and promotes diversity and models a culture of equity, inclusion and respectful exchange for the benefit of all who work, study, live and visit here.

About the Office of Compliance and Campus Climate

Created in 2012 and reporting directly to the President of New Paltz, the position of Executive Director for Compliance and Campus Climate will oversee and guide the institution's compliance efforts on affirmative action, equal employment opportunity, civil rights (Title VII), Title IX, and state ethics. This position will partner with campus leadership to provide training, outreach and opportunities for conversation so we may grow in our commitment to respect, equity and inclusion. The Office of Compliance and Campus Climate will work with student leaders to identify opportunities for productive inquiry that models respectful behavior and engagement, helping to prepare them for responsible citizenship beyond the university. The Executive Director will oversee investigations and bring to appropriate resolution claims of discrimination or harassment under Title VII and Title IX.

Compliance with Title IX and Title VII is fundamental to a vibrant intellectual/creative public forum that reflects and celebrates the diversity of our society and encourages and supports active participation in scholarly and artistic activity.

Title IX Coordinator

The Title IX Coordinator will serve as a strategic guide in identifying and/or assigning appropriate institutional efforts and resources to investigate and address reported incidents of sex- or gender-based harassment, discrimination or violence. The Title IX Coordinator will work with a variety of offices to proactively educate, train, and empower the members of the SUNY New Paltz community to meet both the requirements and spirit of Title IX.

Donald P. Christian, President

- Appendix B: Letter to New Paltz faculty, staff and students:

In my inaugural address, I outlined the following as a critical goal for the New Paltz campus: create a campus climate that is increasingly inclusive and equitable. That goal underscores our mission of educating all members of the College to live in and contribute to a diverse global society, and to ensuring equitable opportunities for success for each member of the New Paltz community. One concrete step toward this objective was the formation in June 2012 of the Office of Compliance and Campus Climate and the hiring of Tanhena Pacheco-Dunn, Esq., the College's first Executive Director of Compliance and Campus Climate. The direct reporting line of this position to the College President underscores the centrality of this work.

The Executive Director's responsibilities include:

- *serving as primary contact and compliance officer for Title IX issues of sexual assault, sexual harassment, and workplace violence;*
- *overseeing our affirmative action plan including reviewing and approving search plans in an effort to diversify our workforce;*
- *handling compliance and ethics oversight as well as other state and federal reporting requirements;*

- *and developing and implementing educational training and programming on equity and inclusiveness.*

The Executive Director of Compliance and Campus Climate works with the entire campus community to advance these goals and objectives. In part, this position will meet a federal mandate that campuses have a single point of contact and resource for the above Title IX complaints, however the broader responsibilities of the position create opportunities to shape and impact campus culture.

As we learned in the aftermath of the posting of racially offensive material on campus in fall 2011, even communities such as New Paltz that are known for their diversity must address issues of race and racial equity – and other dimensions of diversity, equity, and inclusiveness. The forum, "Can We Talk About It," held in November 2011 was the first step in an effort to heal the wounds opened by that incident, and pointed out the need for continued examination and discussion of these important topics on our campus and in our society. The student-planned and – led TRANSactions event held in spring 2012, programs being planned by the Student Association during spring 2013, and discussion of the experiences of LGBTQ students and employees are continuing those conversations.

The new Office of Compliance and Campus Climate and the Executive Director will play a leadership role in this work.

Donald P. Christian, President

End Notes

[1] America's Survival, Inc. has published two books, *All the Dupes Fit to Print,* by Professor Paul Kengor, and *The Crisis in American Journalism and the Conservative Response,* by Tina Trent and Mary Grabar, which examine problems in journalism and journalism education.

[2] Dr. Tina Trent, *Obama's "Fundamental Transformation" of the United States Financed by Offshore and Secret Money from George Soros.*

[3] http://www.adfmedia.org/files/yaf_ca_complaint.pdf

[4] The list includes Hillsdale College, Grove City College, Liberty University, College of the Ozarks, Patrick Henry College, and Regent University.

[5] http://www.nysun.com/national/leftist-with-obama-ties-speaks-at-suny/71716/

[6] http://www.nationalreview.com/phi-beta-cons/42518/ayers-appearance-prompts-diploma-shredding-candace-de-russy

[7] http://abcnews.go.com/blogs/politics/2012/01/elizabeth-warrens-financial-disclosure-report-reveals-strong-personal-wealth/

[8] https://goldwater-media.s3.amazonaws.com/cms_page_media/2015/3/24/Administrative%20Bloat.pdf

[9] http://www.baltimoresun.com/news/maryland/education/bs-md-university-system-chancellor-raise-20160615-story.html

[10] http://articles.baltimoresun.com/2002-03-31/news/0203310008_1_towson-colleges-and-universities-mansion

[11] http://www.familysecuritymatters.org/publications/detail/ending-racial-preferences-in-higher-educationfinally?f=must_reads

[12] http://www.campusreform.org/?ID=7729

[13] qz.com/602956/these-are-the-books-students-at-the-top-us-colleges-are-required-to-read/

[14] http://www.usasurvival.org/home/docs/who.frank.marshall.davis.pdf

[15] http://www.weeklystandard.com/herbert-the-red/article/1066970
[16] http://explore.georgetown.edu/people/jacksonz/
[17] https://president.uchicago.edu/directory/robert-maynard-hutchins
[18] *The Venona Secrets: Exposing Soviet Espionage and America's Traitors*, by Herbert Romerstein and Eric Breindel, pages 278-279.
[19] http://wgresearch.org/about/
[20] Cliff Kincaid's book, *Global Taxes For World Government,* is available online at www.noglobaltaxes.org
[21] https://www.peacejusticestudies.org/conference/2015
[22] http://www.nytimes.com/2016/07/03/opinion/sunday/there-are-conservative-professors-just-not-in-these-states.html
[23] http://www.usasurvival.org/home/docs/Kengor_Rprt.pdf
[24] See "Leftist 'Historian' Howard Zinn Lied About Red Ties," by Cliff Kincaid, http://www.usasurvival.org/home/docs/howard_zin.pdf
[25] See "The 'Bad History' of Howard Zinn and the Brainwashing of America," By Mary Grabar.
[26] http://www.drjudithreisman.com/archives/Spanier_Analysis.pdf
[27] http://www.newyorker.com/news/daily-comment/is-senator-ted-cruz-our-new-mccarthy
[28] http://www.missiontolearn.com/abolish-colleges/
[29] https://www.edx.org/mitx-micromasters-credential-supply
[30] http://scm.mit.edu/program/blended-masters-degree-supply-chain-management
[31] http://www.omscs.gatech.edu/
[32] ibid.
[33] https://www.coursera.org/university-programs/imba
[34] http://www.pewresearch.org/fact-tank/2015/11/20/40-of-millennials-ok-with limiting-speech-offensive-to-minorities/
[35] https://www.justice.gov/opa/pr/us-departments-justice-and-education-release-joint-guidance-help-schools-ensure-civil-rights
[36] http://www.reuters.com/article/us-usa-lgbt-idUSKCN0Y403J
[37] https://www.thefire.org/disinvitation-season-report-2014/

[38] http://redalertpolitics.com/2016/05/02/banned-campus-newspaper-conservative-students-must-speak/
[39] http://www.counterpunch.org/2009/05/15/king-of-the-hate-business/; http://harpers.org/archive/2000/11/the-church-of-morris-dees/; https://capitalresearch.org/2006/11/the-southern-poverty-law-center-a-twisted-definition-of-hate/
[40] http://www.washingtontimes.com/news/2014/mar/28/editorial-the-fbi-dumps-a-hate-group/
[41] http://oracle.newpaltz.edu/abrupt-debate-cancellation-sparks-discussion-across-campus/
[42] ibid.
[43] http://www.investigativeproject.org/blog/2009/08/pandering-for-saudi-dollars-at-yale
[44] http://nypost.com/2009/11/22/schools-iran-pipeline/
[45] http://www.eagleforum.org/publications/column/chinese-crowding-our-college-campuses.html
[46] https://sites.newpaltz.edu/news/2015/10/suny-new-paltz-will-join-historic-u-s-higher-ed-delegation-to-cuba/
[47] http://www.aim.org/aim-report/blogger-wins-award-named-for-soviet-agent/
[48] https://www.newpaltz.edu/media/womenx27s-gender-sexuality-studies/Spring_2014_Newsletter.pdf
[49] https://jessicapabon.com/about/
[50] ibid.
[51] https://jessicapabon.com/curriculum-vitae/
[52] http://nyuad.nyu.edu/en/news-events/conferences/research-conference-2014/agenda-02-23-14.html
[53] http://www.bostonreview.net/poetry/npm14-heather-hewett-eliza-griswold-afghanistan-women-landay
[54] http://www.bronystudy.com/id8.html
[55] http://www.bostonreview.net/poetry/npm14-heather-hewett-eliza-griswold-afghanistan-women-landay
[56] http://www.mhpbooks.com/the-feminist-bookstores-that-inspired-the-portlandia-sketches/
[57] http://www.nydailynews.com/news/national/investigation-suny-new-paltz-colored-racist-signs-posted-campus-article-1.979135

[58] http://www.newpaltz.edu/ccc/
[59] https://www.newpaltz.edu/ocm/admins/campus_climate.html
[60] http://www.newpaltz.edu/ccc/
[61] http://www.newpaltz.edu/lgbtq/
[62] http://www.theguardian.com/education/2015/feb/06/safe-space-or-free-speech-crisis-debate-uk-universities
[63] http://oxfordstudent.com/2014/11/17/abortion-culture-debate-provokes-student-outrage/

Made in the USA
Columbia, SC
05 February 2018